ADVANCE PRAISE

"*Lead Like an Ally* addresses the implicit biases holding women back in our society. This is an entertaining and informative book that practically teaches men and women to be allies for gender equality together."

— **Linda Babcock**, James M. Walton Professor of Economics and is the former Acting Dean at Carnegie Mellon University's Heinz College of Information Systems and Public Policy

"To strengthen businesses, families, the economy and society at large, men and women must join forces and rid our workplaces of outdated Mad Men-era structures. Through research and experience, Julie Kratz shows how transformational these alliances can be and how to form them. She also shows why making this happen sometimes even requires us to unleash our inner superheroes."

— **Josh Levs**, U.N. Gender Champion

"Julie Kratz applies a novel storytelling approach to an issue many of us are trying to tackle - how to find and be an ally for gender equality. The result is entertaining and actionable, with tools on how to lead like an ally packed into every chapter."

— **Dolly Chugh**, Associate Professor at the NYU Stern School of Business and author, *The Person You Mean to Be: How Good People Fight Bias*

"Very few organizations have mastered gender equality. Kratz's research helps us understand why. The *Lead Like an Ally* manager tool kits help my team to be even more inclusive leaders."

— **Jon Dartt**, Vice President of Sales Delta Faucet Company

"Having allies is critical for gender equality. *Lead Like an Ally* is an entertaining fable of the subtle biases affecting women today packed with tools for positive change."

— **Barb Smith**, Advocating, Connecting and Empowering Women in Business, SVP in Financial Services

"If you're a leader who wants to improve things for women at your workplace, read this book. Seriously."

— **Karen Catlin**, former Technology Executive and author, *Better Allies*

"As a champion of gender equality, I've seen men as leaders struggle with how to improve their organizations. *Lead Like an Ally* has powerful examples and a solid toolset that will help any leader look more objectively at their organization. It also provides the how-to's to help leaders start changing their own behaviors and build a culture that gives women more equal standing."

— **Kim Saxton**, Professor of Marketing
Kelley School of Business

"Kratz's latest research captures what is really holding women back at work. For women aspiring to lead, and for all that lead, I highly recommend *Lead Like an Ally*."

—**Deb Hallberg**, CEO of Pass the Torch
for Women Foundation

"This book is for YOU! Julie gives great insights and ideas on how you can take your next step in being an ally for women, and an inclusive leader to all. If you are looking for actionable steps on what an ally looks like, doesn't look like, or how to be an ally, you have found the right resource."

—**Trevor Jenkins**, Diversity, Equality and
Inclusion Leader at ActiveCampaign

"Bravo to Julie Kratz for taking a complex issue and providing practical steps for all of us to be better allies! Diversity is necessary, but inclusion is critical...so we need more inclusive leaders and allies at all levels in order to progress. This guide will help anyone interested in making a positive difference in the workplace and for society at large."

—**Bonnie Fetch**, Executive at Cummins, Inc.

LEAD LIKE AN ALLY

LEAD
LIKE AN
ALLY

A Journey Through Corporate America
with Proven Strategies to Facilitate Inclusion

JULIE KRATZ

NEW YORK

LONDON • NASHVILLE • MELBOURNE • VANCOUVER

Lead Like an Ally

A Journey Through Corporate America with Proven Strategies to Facilitate Inclusion

© 2020 Julie Kratz

Published in New York, New York, by Morgan James Publishing. Morgan James is a trademark of Morgan James, LLC. www.MorganJamesPublishing.com

ISBN 9781642797176 paperback
ISBN 9781642797183 eBook
Library of Congress Control Number: 2019945302

Morgan James is a proud partner of Habitat for Humanity Peninsula and Greater Williamsburg. Partners in building since 2006.

Get involved today! Visit
MorganJamesPublishing.com/giving-back

CONTENTS

FOREWORD

Brad Johnson & David Smith, Authors of *Athena Rising: How and Why Men Should Mentor Women*

We are raving fans of leading organizational consultant, Julie Kratz! For years, we have admired her innovative strategies for developing allies in the workplace. Her first book on allyship, *One*, is a pivotal manual for the applied practice of male allyship and it has been critically important to our own work focusing on inclusive cross-gender mentoring. *One* serves as a one-stop guide for everyday men who genuinely want to lean in to advocacy, accomplice, and ally roles with women to make the workplace more equitable and effective for everyone. As important as it is for grassroots, everyday dudes to be more aware and intentional about allyship for their female colleagues, it is just as crucial that leaders develop a clear understanding of gendered obstacles in the workplace and how they can leverage their leadership roles to crush them.

Enter, *Lead Like an Ally*! This new book by Julie Kratz is a profound gift to leaders of all stripes. Like *One* before it, *Lead Like an Ally* is a terse, pithy, extraordinarily practical guide to both understanding and overcoming gender bias and systemic sexism in the workplace. But this time, Kratz tailors her evidence-based consulting wisdom for managers and executives. After all, gender inequity and lack of full inclusion is ultimately a leadership problem—not a women's issue.

In a stroke of creative brilliance, Kratz frames *Lead Like an Ally* as a riveting fable grounded in the all-too real traditional workplace. Each of the six short chapters, begins with a first-person account of the many real-world gendered hurdles, pitfalls, and insults ubiquitous for women in the modern workplace through the eyes of Jane. Smart, analytical, and emotionally intelligent, Jane is an archetype for what we call a Rising Athena—a bright, talented young woman in a work landscape created by and for men. Jane is simultaneously the name of Julie's young daughter. This truth makes *Lead Like an Ally* all the more compelling. Here is a luminary in the field of inclusion and allyship offering a guide for leaders on how to create a workplace that will one day be more hopeful, equitable, and inclusive when Julie's own Jane arrives at work.

Of course, this inclusive workplace will be a better place for everyone to work and thrive as their authentic selves.

Lead Like an Ally deftly covers all the ally bases. Readers will lean how to clean up the culture, stretch talent equally, establish ally networks, manage meeting behavior, promote belonging, and measure progress toward achieving inclusion milestones. Each chapter includes sections on salient ally insights (takeaways about the experiences of many women in male-centric workplaces) and ally ideas (excellent strategies for solving gender exclusion, bias, and sexism to increase a sense of belonging among women and bolster the organizational bottom line in the process). Finally—listen up here guys—Kratz finishes each chapter with a manager took kit. Yes dudes! There are tons of tools here! This is a veritable leader toolbox for successfully ameliorating gender biases and roadblocks and honestly assessing how your own team is doing when it comes to gender inclusion.

Lead Like an Ally is a gift to leaders everywhere. It is instantly the current standard in the fields of allyship and leadership. Read it, apply it, and watch your teams become more inclusive and successful.

W. Brad Johnson, PhD, Professor, U. S. Naval Academy & **David G. Smith**, PhD, Associate Professor, U. S. Naval War College, Authors of *Athena Rising: How and Why Men Should Mentor Women*

INTRODUCTION

Why Fixing Women Is Not Working

If you Google "women's leadership books," you will likely find titles that tout confidence, risk taking, influencing, and negotiation. In my first book, *Pivot Point*, I too identified authenticity, confidence, having a plan, connecting with purpose, influence, and negotiation skills as critical gap areas for women that are necessary to propel us forward. Sadly, progress has been stagnant since it was written in 2015. Since the early 2000s we have been subtly telling women to forget that they are women and to act more like men at work, as if years of gender socialized behaviors, ingrained in us, can be forgotten. Impossible!

In fact, gender is not binary. We are not simply a man or a woman based on our given sex at birth. There is a gender spectrum. Increasingly, people are identifying themselves as gender neutral or non-binary, meaning that they do not identify with being exclusively a man or a woman. We have been socialized to behave in a way that aligns with our given sex, yet that is not the only option. For women, this is problematic, because as a society we favor masculine over feminine traits in the workplace. This explains why it is impressed upon women to set aside their feminine tendencies and to present a masculine front to advance their careers.

On the gender spectrum, femininity brings tremendous value to workplaces, especially when mingled with masculine traits. The feminine traits of collaboration, emotional intelligence, and tempered risk-taking lead to better business results. Asking women to be more like men is counterintuitive. The natural traits that we offer as women complement those of men, truly creating the ideal balance or the yin-yang effect we are after. Masculine traits balanced with feminine traits result in better leadership, higher employee engagement, and better business results.

The Workplace Is Built for Men to Succeed

Workplace rules have been defined by men. Today's workplace still somewhat resembles 1950s-era *Mad Men*: plagued with sexual harassment, women toiling behind the scenes in low-paying positions, socially mandated after-hour activities, and rigid in-office hour requirements.

At the time of writing this book, women only accounted for 6% of CEOs at Fortune 500 companies and 20% of C-suite positions. As I referenced in my second book, *ONE*, this statistic is static and shows no signs of improvement. In fact, McKinsey's latest "Women Matter" report claims the number is receding. Recent female CEO departures signal a retreat from the once coveted leadership helm. Often, women in these positions feel constrained, constantly battling the gender tightrope bias of having to be feminine with the right dose of masculinity. It is exhausting day in and day out. That is the real reason women leave.

Conversely, when the rules are co-defined by women, we all thrive. Education is an area where women have out-paced their male counterparts for years. So why does that success not translate into the workplace? More women than men graduate from college, achieve higher GPAs, and obtain advanced degrees, yet the key leadership positions in law firms and medical institutions are held by men. It feels opposite somehow. Why? What if the rules could be defined equally across genders? Taking this into consideration, the solution that presents itself for us to lead together as allies.

I believe we are stronger together.

What Is Necessary for Positive Change

Instead of encouraging women to be more like men, we need organizations to meet women where they are and build a culture that values gender equality, inclusion, and a genuine sense of belonging for everyone.

Critical mass is achieved when women make up at least 30% of a group. This is when underrepresented groups feel a sense of belonging and do not feel alienated being the "only" in the room. One or two token women are not enough to make a difference. While 50% is lofty for many leadership teams currently hovering around 20%, 30% is much more achievable. The chances of women speaking up, being heard, and having influence maximize when this is achieved.

This is why I recommend the following ideas to organizations looking to advance gender equality:

1. **Clean up the culture.** Start with the cultural values of the organization and make sure they are inclusive to all genders. Male language is everywhere. Map out the employee experience and think about both vantage points from recruiting, interviewing, onboarding, performance management, pay, promotions, and separation. Bias creeps in everywhere. I recommend treating this as seriously as any business process. Map out the key areas of your employee experience today and where you want it to be, then brainstorm how to fill in the gaps with a strategic road map of activities. Improving the employee experience has a direct correlation on the customer experience.

2. **Stretch talent equally.** Studies show women do not get as much constructive feedback or access to challenging assignments as men. Men are often judged on

their potential, whereas women are critiqued on their performance. In addition, as a woman becomes more successful, she is judged to be less likeable, while the opposite is true for men. This is illustrated by the fact that women, unlike men, typically are rated in performance reviews based on personality traits. It is important to evaluate your organization's performance management data and mine it for gendered language, do a feedback comparison, and evaluate growth assignments by gender. Chances are, you will find gaps that you will need to close and educate managers on, especially middle managers, who have a huge influence on these decisions. These "little" decisions add up.

3. **Establish ally networks.** We now know that organizations that engage men as allies from the top down close the gap much more quickly—three times more quickly, in fact, according to the experts at Boston Consulting Group. This means educating men and women on how to be allies for each other, and promoting cross-gender mentoring, sponsoring, and coaching relationships. Women need safe places to be vulnerable, share stories, come together, and talk about how we work together as allies too. Being an ally is a journey, and organizations with inclusive leadership and ally education programs achieve more.

4. **Manage meeting behavior.** "Man-terruptions" and mansplaining are still pervasive in today's workplace.

Women are far more likely than their male counterparts to be interrupted in meetings. These microaggressions or small incidents—taking credit for an idea, over- or underexplaining an idea, and exclusionary body language toward women—signal that women do not belong and take a big toll over time. This is really why women leave their jobs. I recommend monitoring meetings for these behaviors. Hold leaders accountable for ensuring inclusiveness in meetings by making sure everyone participates, commitments are documented, and note-taking roles and leaders are diversified.

5. **Promote belonging.** Abraham Maslow introduced this theory in his 1943 paper "A Theory of Human Motivation." It is so relevant in today's workplace. Once our basic needs (air, food, water, shelter, security) are met and we feel psychologically safe, the next need we seek is to belong. As women, we do not have that many female role models to look up to. Be sure to equally engage men and women leaders in speaking roles and ensure they are equally recognized in the organization. It is important that men and women are both acknowledged for success of the organization. Increase visibility of women leaders and model what good looks like for others finding their way.

6. **Measure success.** This means paying attention to the numbers of women at each level of the organization, tracking the number of hires, promotions, and exits

and pay gaps by gender. It also includes measuring inclusive values and behavior alignment through employee engagement data and performance review data. If your organization's leadership teams do not reflect your customer base, you are in trouble. You cannot be anticipating the needs of your customers if you do not mirror your customer base. We measure all kinds of important data in business, like profits, engagement, and customer satisfaction. The same should go for gender equality. Consider metrics like applications, hiring, promotion, and separation and hold leaders accountable to them. Finger pointing is commonplace, but it's hard to run from data.

I believe we learn best from our own ideas. To help you formulate your own ideas, I am going to tell you a story of a woman who works in today's workplace, detailing her experiences, with insights and ideas on how an ally could have made it better for her. It is based on the treasure trove of stories I have personally collected in my 15-year career of speaking, consulting, and training leaders on equality and inclusive leadership. It is personal for me, because I am telling it through the eyes of my daughter, Jane, as if she were in the workforce today. I hope this story remains a fable, one that she never has to live. Without further ado, meet Jane.

Chapter 1

CLEAN UP THE CULTURE

I t was the best time of my life and it was the worst time of my life. Everything was happening so quickly.

I was 22, a senior in college, graduating with honors and interviewing for my first real job. I was excited for the future and yet scared of leaving my past behind. I was ready to do something rather than merely study theory; I wanted to make a difference in the world. I had a brain full of information that was ready for action.

Torn between the past and the future, I walked into the career services office. Today was a big day. I had a second interview at a large technology company that was high on my list of dream jobs. It would require me to relocate to Chicago, but that was okay; it was time for change. I would grow to love the windy city.

I took my seat in the waiting room. My mind wandered as I waited. I did not get nervous for interviews anymore. After all, I already had one offer and was waiting to hear back on another offer. I had a good feeling about it.

"Jane."

I was surprised to look up and see it was a woman calling me back for my interview. Strange, this would be the first woman to interview me on campus. Interviews at the other two companies had been conducted by men. I had noticed when I went for onsite interviews that nearly all the interviewers were, in fact, white guys. Well, except for the occasional woman in human resources or marketing.

My mom told me that the women's rights movement had fixed many of the problems facing women at work, that I had an equal chance as men and could do anything. I just needed to be smart and the opportunities would find me. From what I had experienced so far, I could not help but fight off a feeling that maybe she was mistaken. I certainly did not see a lot of women at the companies where I was interviewing, which was strange because at Indiana University, where I studied business, more than 50% of students were female. Walking into the interview, I wondered to myself, where did all the women go?

The woman interviewing me introduced herself as Samantha. She was tall, had her hair neatly tucked back, and walked a fine line between dressing like one of the boys in tech and being feminine. She wore a loose-fitting blazer with a blouse nicely tucked into her designer jeans. It was refreshing to see a woman dress femininely. Unlike one of the other companies where I interviewed, where I met a female vice president. Lyrics from the Aerosmith song "Dude Looks Like a Lady" came to mind. She was overtly masculine in appearance with a very boxy suit jacket and tidy glasses to hide behind. Needless to say, the interview did not go well. It felt like we were both trying to be people we were not. I was playing a part I did not know how to play.

Samantha asked me the usual interview questions.

"What are my strengths and weaknesses?" I thought, *I could say anything, without context, why does this matter?*

"Where do I see myself in 5 years?" I wondered, *Who even knows the answer to that question? It is five years away!*

"Tell me about a time when you solved a problem, analyzed data, worked with a difficult team." My confidence grew; I had these stories ready to go.

The interview was wrapping up, and I felt good going into my close. I had practiced it a million times in front of the mirror and it rolled right of my tongue.

"I am most excited to work for your company because I see myself as a leader. I believe I can grow best in a culture focused on growing top talent."

I was truly excited until I asked Samantha to describe the company's culture. In her response I noted several disingenuous phrases, like "results are king," "we value persistence and a strong work ethic," and my personal favorite, "we are customer obsessed." Although I could not put my finger on what was troubling me at that moment, I had that feeling in my stomach like something was off. I was given the impression that I would have to work like a "warrior," one tech solution at a time, to fit in and be valued.

She must have seen the grimace on my face, because she then shared that they really value diversity and were actively focused on recruiting female talent, but it was just so hard to find. I knew this was not true, personally knowing many young women and people of color actively pursuing careers in tech. I wanted to state the obvious: you are not looking hard enough.

Samantha straightened her glasses and gave me a sincere look. I sensed she wanted to connect with me. She shared her own career story: how she was recruited from a Midwest college similar to mine, worked in engineering for some time, then was encouraged to move into HR to focus on recruiting. She was happy for the opportunity to be on innovative projects early on and missed working with customers directly, but the hours were long and required travel. She had been offered this position because the company wanted to keep her, for they had seen many women leave due to travel and long hours. It seemed to me that she saw me as a younger version of herself as she shared her story.

Her story struck a chord. "So, tell me about the team I would be working with," I said.

She described them as fun, energetic, super hardworking, the "work hard, play hard" type. The team has frequent happy hours and table tennis tournaments, participates sports recreation leagues, and makes a point to hang out both at and outside of work. Those activities did not sound fun to me. It will be important for me to connect with the members of the team and build trust, but would I have to jump through these hoops to achieve that? Definitely food for thought.

After wrapping up, Samantha walked me out of the interview room down the narrow hallway, and thanked me for my time. Her face told me all I needed to know. Run away. You don't want to work here. You do not want to be me someday.

I appreciated her discreet honesty. She had painted a picture that I did not want to be part of. This prompted me to wonder about my other job offers. Were they being honest with me? Or is this the reality of positions in tech for women in general? I had to dig in and learn more.

Once at home I combed the prospective companies' websites. Each highlighted images of diverse looking employees and customers smiling. It was almost too perfect. Then, I dug into my online networks. Who did I know inside these companies? Who could I connect with to learn more?

I reached out to an alumna at ABG, the consulting firm I had an offer from. Nina was happy to take my call. I asked her to share her experience at ABG. She started with the positives—how important the work is, how dedicated everyone is—and then she sputtered, "But I do not feel like I belong there."

Her words hung in the air for what felt like forever. I asked her to explain more.

"I mean, over the past two years, I have been asked out by most of my male colleagues. I am not included in male-only travel and am dissuaded from pursuing principal and partner roles. When I am with clients, I am often asked to take notes and grab the team coffees. Frequently, there is the assumption I must be in HR or marketing."

I was shocked. Nina was wicked smart, at the top of her class, and it sounded like she was not being given the respect that I knew she deserved.

I had to ask, "Would you take the offer if you could do it all over again?"

She contemplated her answer for some time. I could tell she wanted me to make my own decision.

"It is a really great experience. I am so thankful for the opportunities I have been given here. It is a great place to start your career. Maybe just not to grow. I am looking for other opportunities and have found some amazing organizations that are more aligned with my purpose, have more women and different ethnicities working there, and whose cultures truly include everyone, not just the dudes."

I thanked Nina for her time and candor. Wow, today had been a wakeup call. I remembered my mom's words rolling around in my head. Things are different now. My generation paved the way for your generation to succeed."

Why would she mislead me? So, I called her.

My mother was a bra-burning feminist, a hippie, once upon a time, turned corporate taskmaster. Her career pla-teaued when she had children and decided that caretaking was more important than staying late and kissing her boss's ass. She said it was her choice, but I always felt guilty for her not doing what I knew she was more than capable of. She was stronger and smarter than most of her colleagues, and she could be doing so much more for the organization than what her middle manager role granted her.

"Hi, love," she greeted me on the other side of the line.

"Mama, I have to talk to you about something weird that happened today."

I described the happenings of my day, filling her in on Samantha and Nina, and my fear that I would hate corporate America. She knew just what to say to calm me down.

"Jane, you do not like change, and there is a lot at play. You will get through this, just as you have before. Remember when you were deciding on colleges? It is like that but bigger. You are on the right track with your research and are lucky these women are being honest with you, for they did not have be so candid. Back in my day, sexual harassment was considered normal. It sounds to me that you have an ally in both organizations who will help you. The workplace has been built by men, for men to succeed. That is just how it is, so please don't take it personally. Change takes time. You've got this!"

After imparting her wisdom on the matter, she said her goodbyes and was off to save the day at another meeting. Superwoman in action!

That night, as I lay in bed, I thought, this cannot be true. These women have to be making this up, but why would they lie? There was zero incentive to do so. Perhaps, they did not want me to make the same mistakes they had, a true testament to their experiences in working for companies that did not appreciate and recognize the unique value they had to offer. My mom was right; I did need to be more patient, but at what cost?

It had been a long day, full of interview nerves and thinking about my uncertain future. I was the kind of person who always knew what I wanted and had made the right decisions up until that time. I was sailing into uncharted waters. Was I going to make a decision that I would regret?

The next morning, Samantha called with good news. The offered me the position but wanted my acceptance within 48 hours. I knew I needed to buy more time to weigh my options, so we agreed that I would let them know within the week.

To make matters more difficult, a third offer came through. I felt so conflicted. I was fortunate that I had options but unsure of which would be the right choice. I had a difficult decision to make that would impact the rest of my life. What was most important to me: culture, experience, or career growth? I suddenly did not know.

Whenever I do not know what to do, I call Jake, the voice of reason. We have been friends since fourth grade, and he is the first to call me out on my bullshit. It is like he is an invisible mirror that reflects to me my full truth. He sees what I cannot see. I texted Jake, "Can you talk?"

Five minutes later I had my ally on the line. Just like in *Who Wants to Be a Millionaire?* he was my phone-a-friend lifeline. We went through the three options and analyzed the pros and cons and discussed what we knew and did not know. There were a lot of uncertainties. He asked me for my gut instinct. Samantha at the tech firm had a really big impact on me; I did not want to be her when I grow up. Strike. ABG offered unparalleled consulting experience. I knew from Nina that I could get more exposure in two years there than I could in any of the other offers. The third offer came from a great mid-sized company that was growing, yet their reputation was that it would be a long climb up the corporate ladder. I did not know if I wanted to stay somewhere for my entire career like my dad did. He led a team in manufacturing for 30 years and always seemed unhappy when he talked about work.

There seemed to be no right answer, and I wanted the decision to be made. I had hopes of finishing the last two months of college having fun and dreaming about my future dream job. Yet it seemed like all of my hard work had led me to choices I did not know how to make.

Jake brought me back to reality: "Are you seriously complaining about having three great job offers, Jane?"

"No, I am just not as excited as I thought I would be about any one of them. I feel like I have to pick between culture, experience, and growth. Why can't I have it all?"

I was determined to make the perfect decision, so I slept on it. All night I dreamed of scenarios at future workplaces, which included me having success with clients, celebrating with teammates, learning to play table tennis, and fending off unwanted coworker advances.

It was time to make a decision. And, the decision was…

***

Leading like an ally is a journey, and there is no perfect ally.

At the conclusion of each chapter, I will share lost chances to be an ally and what you can do to avoid making these mistakes. I offer my insights into what went wrong, ideas for your organization to lead like allies, and an actionable manager tool kit.

Lead Like an Ally Insights

Being an ally is a journey, and organizations with ally curriculums have better business results. Did you catch these insights?

- **The interview teams were not diverse.** It is common for organizations to send Caucasian men or a token HR woman to recruit. This signals early on to diverse talent that they might not belong. People want to see themselves reflected in the organization's leadership and want to see relatable people succeeding.

- **Women dressed like men.** Cultures where an emphasis is placed on masculinity can set a tone that promotes attire and behavior that is overtly masculine. This can hold minority groups back from being their full selves at work. All too often, this skewed culture signals to women that you have to be more masculine to fit in. There is value in having both feminine and masculine traits. We lose yin-yang benefits when masculine traits dominate.

- **The cultural values used primarily masculine language.** Core values that use phrasing or words like *customer obsessed, warrior,* or *ninja* are known to dissuade women from applying or accepting roles. The words we use matter, especially when these words signal that women have to be like men to succeed. This in addition to the fact that 20–30% of employees identify as gender non-binary creates an increasing need to filter the language we use in organizations to be more inclusive to all talent.

- **Women helped, yet they missed the mark to be allies for women.** There is a perception in the workplace that all women should be helping one another, that women's problems are for women alone. Just as Jane is an enthusiastic beginner ready to climb the corporate ladder, she encounters a cascade of disgruntled women with bad experiences. While Nina and Samantha were somewhat honest about their experiences, they held back, likely because no one had helped them and did not have the time to spend time fighting the battles of other women. There is a bias women have toward other women called the tug-of-war bias. Essentially, the idea is to keep your head down and suck it up, and you will be rewarded. Women with this mentality are missing the chance to be true allies.

- **Women were not included.** This has become so common in today's workplace that it has become very difficult to notice. Whether it presents itself as being overlooked for critical projects, opportunities, and promotions or the employer not accommodating travel for the only woman on the team, women are conditioned to believe they aren't valued and do not belong. All too often the assumption is that HR and marketing are the only areas where women belong. Not surprisingly, these are positions that require the skills that women are often superior to men in: emotional intelligence, collaboration, and balanced risk taking.

Lead Like an Ally Ideas

- **Diversify your interview teams and interview slates to reflect who you want to hire.** Diversify your recruiting and interviewing teams. That means more than just one diverse representative on a panel to avoid tokenism. Evaluate your candidate selection criteria to ensure a diverse talent pool, and set firm expectations with recruiters on what a solid slate looks like.

- **Encourage people to be their full selves at work.** It is not okay to have a culture where everyone looks the same, dresses the same, and acts the same. The best innovation and growth happens with people who look and act different. While we naturally gravitate to others who resemble ourselves and who we feel comfortable with, growth happens when things are uncomfortable. Encourage non-binary attire in the workplace and model it for the team. Paint a picture of what acceptable attire is and provide feedback to employees that emphasizes the importance of being their full selves.

- **Take a hard look at your cultural values.** Cultural values are the nonnegotiable behaviors expected of the team. They determine hiring and separation criteria. It is not okay to have a set of values that favor only one set of people. Review your values and behaviors to identify if they reflect more male or aggressive language; if they do, revise the value and get input to be more inclusive as a team. Take it a step further by mapping out the employee experience, beginning with recruitment through to hiring, promotions, pay increases, and separation. Be sure your organization is living these values every step of the way and that decisions reflect the diversity you want to include in your workplace culture.

- **Promote a culture of allyship.** Women are not the only ones available to help other women. Embody a culture of allyship that encourages men to advocate for, promote, and support women of all ethnicities. Involving only 50% of the population will solve only 50% of the problem. Engage both women and men by implementing a non-bystander policy: if you see something, say something, and hold men and women equally accountable to support women and under-represented groups.

- **Include women at all levels of the organization.** Lack of awareness often leads to the unintentional decision not to include women in out-of-work get-to-gethers and activities such as retreats, sports events, or happy hours. Being left out is a big deal, especially if work-related business is discussed. Consider the impact of these decisions and determine if your organization is being inclusive. If not, check in with your team and review diversity in meetings by questioning who is there and what perspectives you are missing.

Manager Tool Kit

You do not have to reinvent the wheel as a manager. There are excellent resources to support you in your inclusive leadership journey. Inclusive leaders talk candidly about diversity, equality, and inclusion.

Today's employees want to work for inclusive companies. Inclusive companies that have inclusive cultures and leaders promote an environment where people can be their full selves at work. Think about the following questions with your team, rate your top strengths and weaknesses, and brainstorm on how to clean up your culture using the ideas presented in this chapter. It is rare to find a company that is doing all of these things right all of the time.

On a scale of 1–5 (1 = strongly disagree, 2 = disagree, 3 = neutral, 4 = agree, and 5 = strongly agree), how would you rate your agreement with the following statements about your team right now?

- Our meetings have many diverse perspectives, and people represent different backgrounds, races, and genders.
- When someone is treated disrespectfully, someone on our team speaks up.
- Our cultural values are representative of our team and the team we want to be.
- We all feel included in our culture.
- We diversify both interview slates and recruiting and interviewing teams.
- We all have the opportunity to be our full selves to work.
- Everyone is equally included in team-related offsite activities.
- We have a culture of allies where women and men equally support one another.
- We have attire guidelines that permit people to dress according to their gender preferences.
- We are accepting of non-binary genders in our workplace.

You can take the online quiz at www.nextpivotpoint. com/resources.

Chapter 2

STRETCH TALENT EQUALLY

I decided to go to ABG. What did I have to lose?

My dignity, for starters.

The last two years have been a roller coaster. The first six months were awesome. Then, subtle things started to happen, and I realized that Nina had been right. She left shortly after I started, which came as no big surprise.

The first setback was realizing that everyone else in my leadership development program had been given a higher starting salary than me. To add insult to injury, after two years, I learned that everyone else in my program had received a promotion because they had simply asked for it. When I questioned the salary and promotion decisions, I was told to be patient and the opportunities would present themselves. Meanwhile, I had a much higher utilization rate and overall client satisfaction than five of the seven men who were promoted ahead of me. I was livid.

I stayed the course, was patient, and focused on working harder to prove myself. My mother's words rang in my ears as I drove to work almost daily: "Be patient, Jane."

As I got ready to step out of the car to go into work one Monday morning, I looked down at the pavement cracks, took a deep breath, and paused. I was not ready to go in to work. I closed the door and reflected on what I was thankful for. Dave, my leadership coach, had given me some solid advice in our last lunch meeting. Slow down. Build transition time in to your day. When you enter a meeting or get in to and out of your car, spend five seconds being present in the moment. Stop thinking about the past and the future and practice gratitude. It has helped me tremendously to be present and manage the tsunami of emotions I have been feeling at work lately.

I am fortunate to have Dave. The company decided to hire an external coach for me to work on myself as a leader. They deemed me "high potential" but said I had some rough spots that I need to work out to be considered as a rising leader at the firm. Dave was a retired white male executive who had had a glorious career in consulting. I could relate to him on some fronts: clocking my hours with the "always be billing" mentality, pleasing impossible clients, and the high that comes with solving a strategic business problem. Conversely, I was wired to prefer tasks over people and therefore had to work on the relationship part of business. Enter Dave.

During one of our coaching sessions I had stated, "People are so much harder to manage than projects."

Like a good coach, Dave smiled, sank back in his chair, and asked a clarifying question: "How so?"

These simple questions always made me think. I explained, "Clients change their minds. One day, they want this; the next, that. I cannot make everyone happy. My job is to solve their problem."

Dave dug deeper. "So people are a part of business. If you wanted to hone your people skills, what would that look like?"

Back in my car, preparing to enter the office, I found myself power posing (also known as the Superwoman pose) in my car when I saw one of my co-workers in my rearview mirror. I hoped he did not see me. I can only imagine what he would have thought I was doing. I always feel better after I take five. I had reflected. I had paused. Now, it was go time. And, with that, I was up the stairs, entering the office like a human tornado, racing to my seat to fire up my laptop. If I got the conference call started in time, I could spare an extra minute to get a cup of coffee. As I was filling the coffee, Dave entered my mind again.

I was introduced to Dave after I had gotten some strange feedback from my manager, Charles. Charles had stated that I was being "too aggressive and emotional" at work. Charles was one of the few African American leaders and well respected in the organization. I, too, admired him, but his feedback stung. He told me the opinion had come from two of my clients on my last project's feedback form. He was not lying but simply sharing the cold, hard facts. Nonetheless, I did not receive it well.

My first response was defensive: none of my male counterparts had been given this feedback for similar behavior. For example, two of my colleagues, Matt and John, were often called the "Matt and John Show" for repeatedly overtalking people at meetings and freely sharing their opinions. They were commonly accepted as hotheads who blew off steam when things got stressful at work. People made excuses for them, accepting their behavior as "boys being boys."

Why was this an issue only when it was relative to me? Why was I not permitted to behave the same way?

Then, I remembered something my grandmother had taught me: assume positive intent. Assuming that Charles was trying to help me and that he was likely coming from a good place helped to quiet the fear that the whole company was against me. Certainly, he wanted me to succeed. In fact, it was probably harder for him to share the feedback than to just ignore it. A manager who did not care would not tell me the tough stuff. They might be inclined to sweep it under the rug. So, looking at it my grandmother's way, perhaps this was an opportunity to learn. Still, my ego was bruised. I wanted to be right, and It hurt to be wrong.

I had lost my grandmother the previous summer. She had been the glue of our family. We had not been the same since her passing, for she had kept us all together. My mother was still processing the grief and would change the subject when memories of her came up. I wanted to remember her.

She was 95 and lived an amazing life. I realized that in sharing her stories she had told me a lot more about herself than she had shared with others. For instance, I knew that she had worked on the shop floor of a manufacturing plant during World War II as a machinist. She and many other women took the jobs of men while away at war, and then swiftly lost their jobs once the men returned home. She had shared such purpose and connection in that work and had never quite found a way to express herself after that. She was quiet and kept pace with my grandfather, who ruled the household with an iron fist. You did not disagree with him. Perhaps I inherited some of his style, too. Mama used to say that they will never make another one like him. I am proud to have a lot of both of them in me.

I am thankful that I have the courage to speak up, but somehow it has become a problem. Funny, it never was before. I was so outspoken in college, now I have to be quiet and patient. Why?

Time for work. T-minus five minutes until my meeting started, and I had zero energy. I needed caffeine stat.

As I waited for my clients to join the conference call, I sipped my coffee, which surely should be growing hair on my chest by now. I considered my first two years on the job to be net positive. Sure, I had gotten some confusing feedback. I felt like I had to change myself to fit in here, but I had been deemed a high-potential employee, was getting great coaching to improve myself, and had allies all around who cared about me and my career.

Not everyone is an ally, though. As if on cue, my peer Rachel blasted into the office with a smirk and a cocked head. She exclaimed, "I sold it! We got Riverside Health Care!"

Everyone jumped to their feet and ran over to Rachel, high-fiving and hugging her. I sat quietly on my call. Really? Did she always have to outdo me?

Looking back, we were constantly competing for the team's attention. When I had the spotlight, she found a way to shift it back to her. We had started the same day, had nearly identical experiences to date, and were both in line for the next promotion. Only she saw me as her competition, not her ally. Team members acknowledged the tension between us. Some called it the cold war. I chose to rise above it.

I wrapped up my conference call with the client. I talked them off the ledge as usual, put my earbuds in, and sank into my chair to get my work done. I felt good going home that night. I was doing purposeful work and learning new skills. I had this.

Six months later, Rachel received the promotion ahead of me. Her sales were 10% higher than mine, and she had the advantage of sponsors and mentors rooting for her in the decision-making room. I needed to work on my emotional intelligence and people skills and just work harder to get ahead. She knew how to work the office politics better than me. I needed more allies.

The day I found out, as with most days, my boyfriend, Brad, was ready to talk me off the ledge. He was at my apartment when I got home, with a bottle of wine already opened and a puppy dog look on his face.

He knew just what to say to shift my energy. "You are awesome. I love you so much. That company is so lucky to have you. I started a bath for you. Go on and relax and we can talk about it when you get out."

Brad is biracial. His father is from China and his mother is American. He has a very different perspective on life than I do. Instead of it being him against the world, he is patient, humble, and empathetic—qualities I often lack. He was raised by parents who owned their own small business, and he saw them struggle often. He knew that hard work did not always pay off. He was the yin to my yang. He knew how to talk to me. No one in my life had ever figured out how to get in my head like he did. He was an incredible sounding board.

Sinking into the tub that night, I remembered an old ally of mine. My "mirror" Jake and I had lost touch over the past few years. I wondered what Jake would say if I told him about Rachel and being passed over again, despite my best efforts. Maybe I was not cut out for this job, or corporate America was not meant for me. Whoa, crazy talk! I had a business degree and two and a half years of solid street cred. There was no quitting now, I would forge ahead. If Jake were here, he would help me see all the good things that were happening: reasonable pay increases, new client experiences, and both a manager and a coach who supported me wholeheartedly.

So, why did this lingering thought keep bubbling up like the bubbles in the bath: what the heck is next?

Lead Like an Ally Insights

Being an ally is a journey, and organizations with ally curriculums have better business results. Did you catch these insights?

- **Promotion opportunities were not equal.** Last to be promoted among her male peers, Jane was troubled and feeling like she was overlooked. She checked all of the boxes in her performance reviews and was outperforming her male peers on key statistics, yet she was passed over and told to be patient and that her time will come. Meanwhile, all the signals she was getting from the organization's actions proved otherwise.

- **Feedback was focused on personality rather than performance.** Historically, we judge women on performance and men on potential. This means that we need to see women prove themselves over and over again, while confidence is placed in men to accomplish a task they have never done before. Despite being labeled as high potential, Jane was told to wait her turn for the next promotion and given feedback that she was "too aggressive and emotional." Women are far more likely than men to get feedback on personality traits, such as being "too nice" or "too aggressive." There is little room to navigate the middle of the gender spectrum.

Women are expected to be both masculine enough to be taken seriously and empathetic with others to show they care. It is an impossible tightrope to walk, day after day.

- **Women were less likely to get challenging assignments.** Although Rachel shows us that women do get promoted, it appears to be at the expense of other women. Jane has been coached to stay in her lane rather than being challenged with new opportunities. This further drives home the point that we need women and men to be allies to one another. It is not about gloating about accomplishments and self-promoting to fit in and be rewarded. Pitting women against women is divisive and not helpful.

- **Perceptions of negotiation were not equal for men and women.** When Jane inquired about a salary increase, it was not received well. In fact, men are four times more likely than women to negotiate. Conversely, when women negotiate, they are labeled as "difficult" or "unreasonable."

- **Coaching was helpful, yet not enough.** Jane was not able to select her own coach and was paired with someone the organization wanted her to be more like: an older white male. Although he provided great insight, when women are empowered to select their own coaches, they can select someone more aligned with their needs, and the results are far more successful.

Lead Like an Ally Ideas

- **Map out the employee experience.** Promotion decisions are one piece of the puzzle. Recruiting, hiring, performance management, and separation metrics are essential. Understanding where the problem lies is critical to solving it. Promotion decisions exemplify the behaviors in employees that we want to see more of. If men are being unequally promoted, it signals to women that they are not valued. People need to see themselves reflected in the success of the organization. Challenge the potential versus performance bias that exists in which men are perceived to be more capable, even when they may not have the experience, and women have to manage an experience, sometimes multiple times, before they are viewed as capable.

- **Share the love with feedback equally.** Women are far less likely to get constructive feedback or be given fewer stretch assignments than their male counterparts. To combat this, facilitate candid conversations. Set the expectation that your leaders are open and honest with feedback. Measure the perceptions of that behavior with 360 reviews and employee pulse surveys. Ask employees if their managers have given them constructive feedback this week, for example. Feedback is a gift that should be given at least once a week. Additionally, break out the data by manager and by gender identification if possible.

- **Provide stretch assignments to both genders equally.** Make sure you are sharing the love on challenging assignments. Because we more often see men in riskier assignments, there is a bias that these assignments suit only men. Challenge that assumption. If an underrepresented person is overlooked for a stretch assignment, ask the question "Have we considered A or B person? I saw them do X, Y, and Z and know they are capable of this type of work." Offer your recommendations to those who are underrepresented, as their voices are less likely to be heard in the organization. They need allies to amplify their voices.

- **Be mindful of gender bias.** Most people see women as caretakers and men as providers. This leads to negative perceptions at times for women who negotiate versus their male peers. Gender bias sneaks into many decisions as leaders. Check your bias using the implicit bias test (link in the Manager Tool Kit below) or, better yet, invite your team to take it too and offer a safe place for everyone to be vulnerable and discuss their results. It is free, quick, and insightful. There are many assessment choices, including gender, race, overweight, sexual orientation, age, and ability.

- **Middle managers matter.** Provide managers with tools for coaching and providing objective feedback. Women are far less likely to get access to coaches and constructive feedback than men. Jane is lucky to have a strong middle manager who is respected and whom she respects. Many times, the middle management level of organizations is strained with doing their jobs and managing people. Managing people generally takes a back seat to getting the priority work done. Make a standard that managers allocate a percentage of their time per week to coaching and giving feedback to their employees. Setting clear expectations and providing a feedback and coaching framework helps significantly.

- **Coaching works.** Coaching is one of the most underutilized tools a leader has. Tools like the GROW model (goal, reality, options, will) coupled with active listening, open-ended questioning, and self-discovery skills are game changers for today's emerging leader. Managers do not know what they do not know. Give them the chance to learn a new tool and make coaching a part of the manager job description, and in time your managers will be perceived as leaders when they coach well. If managers truly are stretched thin, hire external coaches, use tools like 360 reviews, and allow each coachee to select their coach to ensure the correct fit.

Manager Tool Kit

You do not have to reinvent the wheel as a manager. There are excellent resources to support you in your inclusive leadership journey. Inclusive leaders talk candidly about diversity, equality, and inclusion.

At your next team meeting, consider the following tools.

Tool 1: Implicit Bias Awareness Discussion

- Step 1: Share the Implicit Bias Assessment link (https://implicit.harvard.edu/implicit) with your team. Ensure that it is anonymous and quick (ten minutes or less). The assessment categorizes bias in six diversity variables (age, sexual orientation, race, gender, overweight, and abilities). Emphasize to the team that everyone has bias in at least one area, and likely several. There are no right or wrong answers; the exercise is about awareness.

- Step 2: Using an existing meeting forum or team discussion setting, ask who would like to share their results. Set the stage for psychological safety. Perhaps be the first to share as the leader. Your vulnerability will be mirrored by the group. Most important, frame the discussion as private and ensure that everyone agrees to ground rules up front to not share what is discussed in the room outside of the room. Make it optional to share, and set specific commitments before the meeting concludes by asking, "What did we decide to do differently (more of, less of, etc.) today?"

- Step 3: Keep the conversation alive by checking in with your team via one-on-ones, development planning, or coaching sessions. Ask them, "What is one thing I can do to support you?" Show them you care, and they will care, too.

Tool 2: Watch "Flip It to Test It"

- Step 1: Share the ten-minute TEDx video at https://www.youtube.com/watch?v=Bq_xYSOZrgU with your team. Ask everyone to come prepared to your next team discussion to share insights, ideas, and challenges with this strategy to overcome gender bias at work.

- Step 2: Facilitate an inclusive discussion where all voices are heard. Ask people to partner up or meet as small teams to ensure that more introverted team members feel safe sharing. Similar to the Implicit Bias Assessment Discussion, reassure the team of psychological safety and maintain an environment with firm ground rules to avoid judgment.

- Step 3: Be brave as a leader and share your own candid experiences of times you have gotten it right and times you have had blind spots to bias. Own your bias and encourage the team to adopt practices to manage their biases.

Chapter 3

ESTABLISH ALLY NETWORKS

Looking in the rearview mirror, I now see that perhaps I was being a tad emotional when things had not gone my way at work. After eight years at ABG, I decided to work for one of my clients. Tri-Go, a pharmaceutical company, was our biggest client, and I really enjoyed consulting with them. They offered me a desirable leadership position with perks I could not refuse. I already knew all of their senior leaders from my project work, and since I started there, they have been great allies for me in my career.

There was a natural fit that I cannot fully explain. I had so much more support than I did at ABG. I enjoyed coming to work. Gone were the days when I had to "take five" before coming in to the office to avoid having a panic attack. I now looked forward to work and Monday mornings. We had a team huddle every Monday over breakfast to plan for the week, and I deeply enjoyed connecting with my team. We talked about our weekends, our families, our hobbies, and our key tasks for the week. I could actually ask for help if my workload was too high without feeling like I was incompetent. I could jump in and help my team without feeling like a micromanager. We trusted each other. We liked to spend time together. We even played soccer outside of work together.

Hindsight is 20/20. I now know what a mess ABG was. There was no unity. We were all independent consultants out to beat each other on our numbers. This realization led to Rachel and I finally clearing the air, thus ending our cold war. I see now that she felt the same way I did. We were pitted against each other unfairly as young, high-potential women. We had been positioned against each other to battle for the one opportunity for a woman to lead. It was a zero-sum game—either I won or she won. It was like there were only so many positions for women to lead. There was no win-win. There was room for only one of us. She too had left ABG, to start her own business, and from what I have heard, she seems to be killing it. I can be happy for her now. We are both in a better place where we can support one another. That culture was the problem, not us. What a relief to know we can work together, as women, instead of against each other.

When Rachel and I went to happy hour together, I shared my exit interview experience. On my last day, they asked what they could have done to keep me longer. I did not give them the real answer. I thought to myself, *Haven't I already shared that? What good would it do?* I wanted to leave on a positive note in case I needed a reference or wanted to come back some-day when they got their act together, so I lied and told them I wanted more flexibility and stability (insert scoff and eye roll). Of those who had left in the previous year, 75% were women and people of color. Clearly, ABG was sending a message that we do not belong. White men continued to advance at a much higher rate than my allies, so when given alternative, of course I jumped on it. Rachel shook her head in agreement.

On day one at Tri-Go I was assigned a mentor, Paige. Paige was from Puerto Rico and had long flowing hair halfway down her back. She was absolutely beautiful, smart and strong, all at the same time. She was mid-career and had a great reputation at the company. She was a director in a critical function and leading growth targets for the organization. I saw myself as her in five years (hopefully). She showed me what good looked like as a woman leader. I was lucky to have her in my corner. We went out to lunch on my first day, and she questioned me about what I wanted for my career and how she could be supportive. No one had ever asked me those questions before. I did not know what to say.

Over the following months, my workload grew, as did Paige's. Despite our monthly standing meeting, we often had to postpone or cancel due to our growing responsibilities. We were both killing it and killing ourselves at the same time. When we passed each other in the hall or had a team meeting together, I felt the same, continued connection. She smiled, encouraged me to speak up in meetings, and asked how I was doing and how she could help. She offered advice, helped me see what obstacles might be coming, and was quick to point out the obvious when I could not see it myself. We both knew she did not have the bandwidth to help any more than that.

After my first year, we gave up on the monthly rendezvous but maintained that tight bond of sisterhood: we had each other's backs. I was quick to defend her and her team and stalked her calendar for windows when I could just drop by. Paige was already mentoring six women, and I did not want to be selfish but to honor the time she could pour into them. That is when it dawned on me that my mentor did not have to be a woman.

I decided to take up another mentoring relationship. I asked myself, *Who do I want to be some day?* And the answer was Paul. Paul was an openly gay white male vice president who was witty, smart, and super-intuitive. He had an amazing presence and had better people skills than I—a sore spot for me, still. Paul knew how to work a room and get everyone to say yes to things that were not popular. I wanted to learn from him, and I thought he could benefit from my analytical perspective as well. My intuition was right. Paul turned out to be amazing at opening doors for me that I could not access myself. He used his white male privilege to help me be seen and heard in ways that I had not been before.

I remember one meeting in which I was presenting an idea for a new line of services that were considered controversial. The leadership team wasn't on board with my approach. Despite my best efforts to present the idea to each leader individually, I got the sense I would get some pushback in the leadership team discussion. Paul said just the right thing in that meeting. When the objections started flying, Paul came to my defense with "What is the worst thing that could happen if we tried it?" and "Let's listen to Jane. She has given this a lot of thought."

As a result of Paul's mentorship, I picked up a sponsor named Steve. Steve was late in his career, very old-school in thought, and had exclusively mentored and sponsored only men. He said that they reminded him of his younger self, but he had taken note of me as I spoke up more, declared my ideas confidently, and self-promoted my accomplishments publicly. After a meeting one winter, he said, "I am impressed by you. I would not have minded working for a leader like you when I was younger." I chose to take that as a compliment. Clearly, he had experienced a shift. I figured, this is my opportunity, take it. So, I asked for one half hour a month to pick his brain in regard to my career. We shook hands on the spot in agreement—it was a go!

What made Steve so great was that he had access to people in the organization that I did not yet have access to. He could influence decision makers very easily by sharing his endorsement of my efforts. He was in the talent management and succession planning meetings where I was being evaluated. I proactively communicated my successes to him in our regular meetings, and he championed me and reinforced those critical talent reviews. Leaders who did not work with me or know me yet knew what I was doing and how well I was doing it.

I am very into personal development. Maybe it was the pregnancy hormones (oh yeah, I was pregnant) or just the need to improve, but I started listening to a lot of podcasts. I stumbled upon one about women in leadership, and I took note this quote from one of the guests:

> Women need allies at work. Especially male allies, as they still make the majority of the decisions and are 80% of leaders in organizations today. Women leaders and people of color are underrepresented in organizations. That is why we need men as allies. Allies help you feel seen and heard, and that you belong.

I took an inventory of my allies and realized I had been doing this unconsciously throughout my career. I had a sponsor (someone who advocates for you), a mentor (someone who advises me and is a future version of myself), and a coach (my manager was a great Yoda-like Jedi mind trick master), and I still talked to my earlier coach Dave from time to time (even though he treats me like his daughter some of the time).

This podcast also helped me understand that not all men are my allies. I did have one nemesis, Robert. Robert loved to put me down in team meetings. He found the one thing I did wrong and pointed it out—publicly, when it is too late to correct it and save face. I was called on the carpet and left with no choice but to say, "I goofed." After it had happened five times, it was clear it was an unlikely coincidence. I decided to approach Paige and Paul and ask for their advice. They both said Robert did not have a great reputation and was harming himself by behaving this way, but they did not offer any tangible solutions to manage the situation.

I saw no choice but to approach Robert directly and have a candid conversation. I went to his office one day when I knew he was available and asked him if we could chat. He agreed and we went for a walk around campus, side by side. I explained to him that I needed to talk about something that was difficult for me to share with him. "You call me out in team meetings."

It hung for about ten seconds. Robert finally said, "Why haven't you told me this before? I had no idea."

We agreed that the next time it happened (which it did, four more times), I would call him on it. He quickly recognized the behavior and curbed it. How I wish I would have talked to him directly before. It could have saved months of awkwardness.

I was approaching mid-career and felt I needed a safe place to be vulnerable and share my story with other women. I volunteered to lead our Tri-Go Women's Employee Resource Group after attending a few events and noticing an opportunity to improve programming and engagement. I had been amazed by the feedback, as women were sharing their stories and supporting one another in ways I never saw at ABG. We were including men as allies, too. I actually invited Robert, Paul, and Steve to come as my allies to the first male allies program. They listened and learned, just like good allies do.

At that time, things at home where chaotic. I was expecting a baby in a few months and my husband, Brad, had just started a new job. I decided it might be time for my career to take a back seat. I loved my job and would return to work full-time once we had both completed our family leave time, but I knew the bulk of the caretaking would fall on me. I would be responsible for the drop-offs and pick-ups due to Brad's longer work hours. I would be the one working from home if the baby got sick. I had seen women really struggle at work with little people at home. They looked like zombies and often said they got little sleep and had little time to do things just themselves. I had not yet seen any examples of successful working mothers.

I would have to do better than that. But how?

Lead Like an Ally Insights

Being an ally is a journey, and organizations with ally curriculums have better business results. Did you catch these insights?

- **Underrepresented high-potential women and people of color left when they felt they did not belong.** Although ABG asked the right questions in their exit interview process, people on their way out are unlikely to give honest answers. There is no upside to critiquing a culture. People just leave and give answers that reinforce the lack of inclusion like "flexibility" and "stability." These are not the real reasons.

- **Women were assigned women mentors.** It is over-taxing to women who are successful to be responsible for mentoring all the other women who want to advance. Paige is great, but when every high-potential woman is given Paige as her mentor, bandwidth becomes an issue. Men are equally qualified to mentor women; however, men tend to mentor those who look like them and act like them. We learn from people who are different from us, whether it is a different gender, race, sexual orientation, age, or ability.

- **Sponsors were more likely to be male.** Men are often in positions of power and influence. Networking studies have revealed that men are 54% more likely to have access to influential people in organizations. While women are strong at relationships in general, men are typically stronger at strategic relationships and knowing the right people who can connect them with opportunities and other influencers.

- **The Women's Employee Resource Group created space for psychological safety.** It is important for women to have a safe place to share their stories and to be heard with just women. It is also critical to have times to invite allies to participate and listen and learn sometimes. As humans, we seek safe environments with people who look and think like us, and having employee resource groups offer a safe place for those underrepresented at your organization.

- **Not everyone was an ally.** Robert is a great example of a nemesis turned ally. Not all people want to be allies for women. Do not expect all men to be allies for women. Candid conversations can help bring men into the conversation.

Lead Like an Ally Ideas

- **Pay attention to code words in exit interviews.** Solid exit interviews ask open-ended questions, like "If you could change anything at our organization, what would you recommend?" or "What are the things that kept you up at night as an employee here?" Real questions get real answers. It is also important to protect the anonymity of those interviewed to ensure there is no retaliation or ill consequences when sharing sensitive information. If there is any issue with individual leaders, it needs to be addressed immediately. Pay attention to which managers are losing good employees and hold them accountable for engaging their employees more.

- **Promote cross-gender mentoring.** Encourage men and women to mentor across the gender spectrum. Whether you have a formal mentorship program or informal networks, make sure gender is not a criterion in matching mentees to mentors. Make it about specific competencies (skills, behaviors, attributes). Match mentors with mentees who are looking to grow in areas where the mentor is strong.

- **Ensure equal access to sponsors.** If men are the primary recipients of talent review discussions, you may have this problem. Open up the sponsoring swim lanes to women and call leaders out if they are recommending or talking only about male talent.

- **Invite allies to participate in employee resource groups.** Women's employee resource groups are often dominated by white women. Ensure you are engaging people of color, the LGBTQ community, and men as allies. Invite them personally to events, and maintain a safe place for women only for some events as needed.

- **Have candid conversations.** Just as Jane did with Robert, a nemesis can turn into an ally. Doing so requires us to talk to the person we need to be talking to, not other people. It is hurtful to have meetings after the meeting to talk about people behind their backs. Go directly to the source and maintain a culture of challenging with care. As a leader, it is critical that you model that we say what we mean without being mean.

Manager Tool Kit

You do not have to reinvent the wheel as a manager. There are excellent resources to support you in your inclusive leadership journey. Inclusive leaders talk candidly about diversity, equality, and inclusion.

Some options to consider are hosting educational events such as these:

- **Lead Like an Ally talk:** We have a talk titled "Lead Like an Ally" with simple, fresh ideas to meet you where you are at on your ally journey. Learn more at NextPivotPoint.com.

- **Women's leadership panel:** Don't have a budget to hire an outside speaker? Leverage the top talent you do have. Get a cross-section of diverse talent from different areas of the organization with different backgrounds. Ask them questions like "What was your career path?" "What barriers have you encountered, and how did you overcome them?" and "Who have been your allies and how have they supported you?" Open it for a Q&A.

- **Lunch and learn:** Get your team together and watch a video or webinar together. TED Talks from Brené Brown, Amy Cuddy, and Adam Grant are also great conversation starters.

- **Book discussion:** There are so many excellent women's leadership reads out there: *How Women Rise, Dare to Lead, What Works for Women at Work, Ask for It, How Remarkable Women Lead, Radical Candor, Athena Rising, Better Allies, Inclusion, Pivot Point, and ONE,* just to name a few. Craft a book summary and questions to drive positive change.

- **Podcast discussion:** Have the team listen to a podcast episode and come prepared to discuss key takeaways and action items together. My favorite gender equality and diversity podcasts are *Tilted, HBR Women at Work, A Will to Change,* and our very own *Pivot Point.*

Chapter 4

MANAGE MEETING BEHAVIOR

"**J**ust keep breathing. Slow and steady. Pretend that you are blowing out birthday candles," my husband, Brad, coached.

"I'll show you how to blow out candles. This hurts!" I exclaimed.

I had been in labor for 20 hours, and little Lucy was not budging. She was hell-bent on staying put, and I was ready to give up and let her. I mustered enough energy for one final push, and out she came, screaming her head off. After the nurse cleaned her off, I held her warm little body to mine and felt instantly connected. Through tears of joy, I met my greatest ally. She was the perfect blend of our skin colors, a nice tan with tight-knit, dark curly locks of hair. Her little eyes were open for her to see the world.

Two days in the hospital passed quickly, and then we were home sweet home, adjusting to our new role as parents. My mom helped the first week, letting me rest and recuperate. Brad had parental leave from his new job for the following two weeks. Their help would see me through until the halfway mark of my six-week short-term disability leave. (Ha! I did not have a disability; I had a baby!) My company did not provide maternity leave outside of FMLA, so my leave was going to be rushed, forcing me to pack all the experiences in early.

I was so relieved that I had had a conversation with my manager before I left. I approached my manager, Scott, at the end of a work day on week 38 of the pregnancy. I knocked on his office door lightly and asked if he had a minute with the usual, "Don't worry, everything is okay." Scott closed his laptop and gave me his undivided attention.

"What's up?" he replied.

I presented my leave of absence plan, explaining that I would be out of the office for a total of six weeks, likely starting in two weeks, but would be checking in occasionally should the team need me. My project work had already slowed down, and I had transitioned my daily tasks to Ken, my peer. Ken was stepping in for me while I was out, and I wanted Scott to know that I was thankful for him. What would I ever do to repay Ken? I carried guilt for burdening him with my work in addition to his own. Over the past months we had cultivated a close friendship at work. He had confided in me that his wife had struggled with postpartum depression, so he totally understood the need for me to take my time. He and his wife had two children, and from our many conversations, I think he secretly enjoyed working more just to get out of the house.

For me, time at home with Lucy was good, a blend of not sleeping, sleeping, cleaning up spit-up, rinse, and repeat.

As my six weeks approached its finale, I reached out to Scott and Ken. Ken reported that everything had gone well, except for a few minor hiccups he had already taken care of. He had kept everything afloat. The reception from Scott was different. He asked strange questions, like "What hours are you going to work when you return? Do you have the capacity to come back so quickly? Who do you have to help?"

My husband had not been questioned this way when he returned to work. I felt as though all expectations were placed solely on me. Lucy has two parents! Aside from nursing, Brad could do anything that I could do for Lucy.

My first day back was reminiscent of my days working at ABG. It was hard to say goodbye to my new little ally, Lucy. I sat in the parking lot, taking deep breaths and thinking of what Dave, my former coach, would say. Lucy was at home with my mother, and even though I knew she was in good hands, I had a lingering feeling that being at home with her was more important than my job. I mustered up the courage to put on my big-girl panties, leave my car, and head into the office.

I was greeted warmly by the entire office. Wow, what a difference that made. Everyone wanted me there. I felt so lucky to work with such an amazing team. Throughout the day, team members checked on me and asked to see baby pictures. People inquired with curiosity: "Wow, she is so beautiful, that beautiful skin. What is your husband?" As if he were a thing.

I responded kindly, "His parents are from China," while correcting them: "His ethnicity is Asian American." They could have asked about his ethnicity or where his family is from to be more inclusive.

The interest in Lucy trickled off by the end of the week, yet that first day made a huge difference in helping me feel good about working again.

Steve, my sponsor, was especially helpful that first week. In the first meeting since my return, I felt very unprepared; Steve started the meeting to give me some time. He then opened it up to me by then asking me softball questions about my opinion on topics I knew well, tapping into my strengths like the all-star ally that he is to me. By the end of the meeting, I felt almost normal again.

I fell into a nice routine over the coming weeks. Brad handled Lucy's drop-off at my mom's in the morning, enabling me to get into work early, and I managed her pickups by leaving work around four p.m. each day. Scott was amazed with my productivity and rated me as "high potential" in my performance review. He said I would have to manage a challenging project to show my leadership skills in order to get the promotion I had my eye on.

That new project was very tough. I was charged with leading a cross-functional team (think dysfunctional team) on a new product launch that had a lot of attention from senior leadership, what is known in the corporate world as a stretch assignment. Women rarely get these assignments, especially those who have small children at home. The project required frequent travel, which I actually enjoyed, but others assumed I would not want to travel after having Lucy. I discovered many solutions that enable working women to still be moms; for example, when traveling, I could pump my milk and ship it home.

At that first product launch meeting, I was calm, cool, and collected. Taking stock of the room, I realized that I was the only woman on the team. Chad was our R&D team member, Doug was from market research, Rejen was from operations, Thaddeus was representing sales, and Scott would be our sponsor. I was outnumbered by a long shot. I had this...or so I hoped.

After coming to terms with my minority status, I learned to lean on my mentor, Paul, for guidance on how to manage my interactions with the team. He helped me navigate what to do when someone interrupts me in a meeting and how to deflect the role of taking notes, and he inspired creative ways to get people to prioritize the meetings rather than show up late or not at all. Paul was quick to offer tips. He was surprised to learn that people were questioning my authority. He had never been questioned as a team leader. I was the team lead, and this product launch was a critical company priority. He couldn't believe that men were blowing me off, for that had simply never happened to him.

He recommended that I rotate the role of taking notes, so that everyone had to take a turn, freeing me up to participate and lead the meetings instead of documenting them. His suggestion was very useful applied at home as well for handling housekeeping and bringing in food. I did not have to do the busy work just because I was a woman, for it would hold me back and limit my visibility. He understood the challenges facing underrepresented people as a gay man in a very straight workforce. People made assumptions about him that were not fair. He saw gender more neutrally because he identified as gender non-binary, exhibiting feminine as well as masculine behaviors.

While I appreciated what Paul did for me, I needed some tough love. Enter Robert, my former nemesis. He stepped into my office (yes, I now have an office with real doors), closed the door, and kindly asked, "Can we talk?"

"Of course. What's up?" I replied, intrigued.

Robert didn't miss a beat. "I have noticed what you are doing while running this new product launch. People aren't paying attention to you, and you aren't commanding the respect you deserve, which makes me question if you have what it takes to make this happen."

"Are you serious, Robert?" was my response.

"Listen, Jane. I have your back, and I believe in you, but I get the impression you are seriously struggling. How can I help?"

Sometimes our allies tell us what we need to hear, not what we want to hear.

It all came flooding out. "I have no idea. They are not listening to me. I feel alone. I do not know what I am doing." The tears swept over my face. I did not know what to do. I was being weak, vulnerable, and downright confused. "I feel like I am in a fog and cannot get out."

"I believe in you," he reassured me. "You have led the team before, and I am confident you can handle this now."

I was so angry for being called out and so happy for his support. I felt scared, tired, and hopeless, yet I was comforted that I had allies who were stepping up for me. I had no choice but to succeed; they expected that from me.

Cue my meditation mantra: I do have this. I am an admirable leader. My team believes in what we are doing together.

I practiced this for six months until I started to feel my confidence grow. As Lucy grew, learning to crawl and talk, my voice grew, too. My fight and her fight were one and the same.

The following meeting with the product launch team went very differently from the first.

Confidently, I opened with: "Together, we are going to set the ground rules. Everyone's voice is heard. Everyone feels included in the conversation. We hold each other accountable and agree to be candid with one another. What else…"

Everyone sat, stunned in silence. No one spoke. Everyone held back.

"Really? No response? You are better than this," I said, breaking the silence.

The team began to chant their responses.

"Respect."

"Fairness."

"Equality."

Basic human traits. They all rallied around it. They wanted to be a team, and I wanted to be their leader. I did not like having to be the only woman, and it appeared that they did not like me being their "fearless" leader. There was common ground to find. I just had to find it and set boundaries around it.

A month went by, and the product launch was quickly approaching. While our sales representatives were in product training, I was inundated with those representatives posing obstacles and resisting the launch. I had already successfully won over my cross-functional team, and I now needed the sales team to follow suit. The battle seemed never-ending. I wondered, if I were a man, would I have to deal with all this resistance? I did not think so. I remembered my mother's words: "Life is not fair." Boy, was she right.

I decided to call on an ally. I swung by Scott's office late in the day toward the end of a grueling training week. We had over 100 sales representatives in town that week, and half of them were firmly resisting selling the new product. Like they had a choice.

Scott was quick to listen and learn as always. He always held space for me to let it all out, while balancing questions and guiding me to find a solution, rather than complain. After listening for ten minutes, he offered, "What do you think they want?"

Oddly enough, I had not been thinking about the problem in that context. I had been wanting to force this new product on them because it was their job to sell it, but what was in it for them? It finally dawned on me, and then like a tidal wave, ideas rushed into my head. Maybe their resistance was because of something other than me? Assuming that it was not about me helped provide more clarity.

"They want more commission on the product because it is harder to sell. The sales process is longer, and they want to speed it up with discounts and incentives that we did not build into the budget. They want different marketing materials that are against our brand standards," I answered.

"What gives are you willing to make?" Scott responded, leaning back into his chair and offering a supportive smile and nod.

"We have some flexibility with our budget. Maybe I could offer some incentives to help them have some quick wins earlier in the sales process. Especially if we targeted the right customer profile, it would show them that we know our market. It could help them prospect and speed up the sales process," I said confidently.

Scott's smile grew. He adjusted the collar on his neatly pressed white shirt and said, "Sounds like you have a plan. I knew you knew what to do. I am really proud of you."

I felt refreshed and grateful to him for guiding me to my breakthrough. I did know the answers all along; he facilitated my change in perspective to unlock them. Maybe the fact that I was so sleep deprived was blurring my vision, making it difficult for me to find my way to a solution. Lucy was keeping me on a tight six-hour sleep schedule, and Brad was helping, but he could be doing more. I needed to take better care of myself and equalize the workload.

I left Scott's office with a plan in mind and ready to go home to enjoy a night with my family. I called the sales leader, Thaddeus, on my way home and asked for his input on the sales objections I was getting and shared my ideas. He jumped on the two ideas I had and thanked me for being so thoughtful. He committed to support my ideas and said he would help get his team on board. He surprised me with the first compliment he had given me since we had begun working together: "I really like working with you. I would love to work for you someday."

I felt a glow wash over me. I had hit my stride. How would I keep this up?

Lead Like an Ally Insights

Being an ally is a journey, and organizations with ally curriculums have better business results. Did you catch these insights?

- **Jane was the only woman in many meetings.** Being the only person who looks like you and thinks like you can be exhausting. Unfortunately, most decisions made today in the workplace are by Caucasian men, who are making those decisions unbalanced by other perspectives and lacking innovative thought. When meeting rooms are full of people who all look the same, think the same, and have the same experiences, the decisions are not as innovative.

- **Women were expected to play a housekeeping role in meetings.** Women are often tasked with cleaning up the room, bringing in food, or taking notes at meetings. These are non-value-added tasks that distract women from the business at hand and reinforce perceptions that women are caregivers and wallflowers to the decisions that are being made by men. Housekeeping tasks hinder workload management and perceptions of leadership for women at work. When women take on more responsibility in addition to their regular work, it limits their capacity and visibility to other opportunities.

- **Jane's authority was questioned.** The cross-functional meeting team members often did not show up or were late to meetings, signaling a lack of respect. While Jane felt like she was leading, the perception was that her team did not respect her as the leader. When she compared notes with her allies, she learned that the men did not share her same experience.

- **Non-inclusive meeting behaviors were tolerated.** Interruptions, taking credit for others' ideas, and limited participation in meetings signal that the meeting and, therefore, the culture are not inclusive. When underrepresented people are interrupted or not given credit for their ideas, they feel excluded and learn to hold back. Good meetings are those where all voices are heard in a productively egalitarian method.

- **Women have a knack for aligning teams on decisions.** Jane thrived as a leader in her ability to rally people to common goals. She triangulated different ideas to build one solid set of goals that the team aligned with. Women tend to outperform their male counterparts in the ability to integrate people and unify teams.

Lead Like an Ally Ideas

- **Set a standard that all meetings must have a diverse perspective.** Make it a cultural norm to have inclusive meetings where people with different backgrounds, functions, ethnicities, genders, abilities, and perspectives are invited. If you are in a meeting that is not diverse, ask, "What perspective are we missing here?" It gets attention and increases the chances of inclusive meetings in the future.

- **Share the love of housekeeping tasks.** From note-taking to office housework, women are more often asked to do these non-value-added tasks. Pay attention to these tasks and who is doing them. If it tends to be more women, point it out. Rotate responsibilities across the team.

- **Set ground rules.** Jane brilliantly did this with her team to have them agree they would be respectful and fair and treat others equally. She facilitated discussion instead of dictating to the team. Leaders who lead like allies get results more quickly through an open dialogue versus a forced approach. No one likes to be told what to do; often we want to come up with our own solutions.

- **Call out bad behavior in meetings.** Meeting behavior is one of the most telling traits of an inclusive team. If not all voices are being heard equally and interruptions, taking credit for others' ideas, and mansplaining are permitted, these behaviors will keep happening. Have a conversation about these behaviors to prevent them from continuing, and call out bad behavior immediately, linking the perception of that behavior and what will happen if it continues. Clearly outline the consequences of bad behavior and hold the team accountable for calling them out. The situation-behavior-impact model is very effective.

- **Create space for women to thrive.** Just as Paul and Scott did, leaders that lead like allies, ask questions and coach women and other diverse groups. They lean into candid conversations with empathy, avoid downplaying diverse people's experiences, and instead, seek to better understand them and facilitate problem solving with self-discovery vs. simply giving advice. Often, modeling inclusive communication with asking vs. telling, actively listening, and promoting self-discovery spreads throughout a culture when all leaders are brought in.

Manager Tool Kit

You do not have to reinvent the wheel as a manager. There are excellent resources to support you in your inclusive leadership journey. Inclusive leaders talk candidly about diversity, equality, and inclusion.

Diversity expert Jennifer Brown says, "Everyone has a diversity story. Even those you do not expect."

As an ally, it is impactful to share your diversity story, even if you are a cisgender Caucasian male with all of your abilities. People will be surprised, and it demonstrates vulnerability, which builds trust.

To craft your diversity story, think about your experiences:

- When you felt like you did not belong.
- When you were different from the rest of the team.
- When you had to minimize or maximize traits about myself to fit in (this is called covering).

Then, write your story down. Start with the beginning. Set the scene with the who, what, where, and when. Build up a climax in the murky middle with emotions and turmoil. Then, conclude with taking perspective and share key takeaways. A good story is two to five minutes long.

Finally, share your story with your team in a group setting or one-on-one. Ask them to think about their story and be open to listening to their experiences, especially if they are a person of color, LGBTQ, or identify as a woman.

Check out my diversity story here: https://disrupthr.co/vimeo-video/everyone-has-a-diversity-story-whats-yours-julie-kratz-disrupthr-talks.

Chapter 5

PROMOTE BELONGING

The product launch catapulted my career. Five years later, I was still wearing that badge of honor proudly. Our product ended up surpassing expectations and beating sales goals for three years before being replaced by a new technology.

Rejen, my former cross-functional adversary turned ally, had moved on to a vice president position at one of our competitors, BioSphere Inc. He had reached out to me to see if I was interested in joining his team. While I was flattered by the opportunity, I did not have any reason to leave. I was at the senior director level, well poised to move into the C-suite in the next five years, given my performance reviews and upcoming retirements. I was willing to wait my turn. Lucy had just started kindergarten, and my son, my little male ally, Cole, was out of diapers and only two years away from being in school full-time, too.

I had a plan for my career, and it fit around my family. Brad had taken a step back at work to support my career by taking on the majority of the household and caretaking tasks. We outsourced nearly everything from groceries to housekeeping to child care before and after school. I was fortunate to have that kind of support. It seemed to me that many of my female co-workers did not have the same support from their partners necessary for the furtherance of their career that I had with Brad. In fact, many had gotten divorced when they were promoted beyond their partners; the shift in balance was detrimental to their partnership. At Tri-Go, the only women at director level or higher did not have children or their partner stayed at home. I was often asked, "How do you do it all?" I wondered if they would ask that question of a male leader. It would seem a bit silly to say that to our CEO.

Rejen was persistent about the job offer. He said it would be a significant promotion and pay increase. We could afford our lifestyle on my income alone. Brad was excited about being with Cole for his last two years at home and encouraged me to think about it. I would have to wait five years at Tri-Go for what was being offered to me right away at BioSphere.

I doubted myself. Was I ready for this opportunity? Did I meet the qualifications? What if I did not succeed?

I ruminated on these thoughts for nearly two weeks before I pulled the trigger. Brad's voice rang in my ears: "What is the worst that could happen?" I had heard about studies showing that men would apply for jobs even if they met only 60% of the qualifications, whereas women wait until they meet nearly all the qualifications. Perhaps I was overthinking this.

When Rejen and I met for coffee, he said all the right things. There was no boys' club. They had 50% women on the leadership team. The board of directors was focused on equality. I would report directly to him as associate vice president of marketing, and there was a great chance I would be promoted to vice president of marketing within two years.

I thought about it for two days before deciding to say yes to Rejen. He exclaimed, "Woohoo!" on the other side of the phone line. The hardest person to tell was Scott. He had been a true ally for me and had done so much by helping me to be seen and heard while coaching me to success. I was afraid he would be disappointed. When I told him, he smiled from ear to ear and, of course, asked a question: "What are we going to do to celebrate? This is good for you."

It was bittersweet leaving that last day with my cardboard box of artifacts accumulated over the years, including my product launch team picture, several top performer awards, and pictures of my family.

After joining BioSphere, the significant increase in my income allowed Brad to leave his job in financial services. He was instantly happier being at home with the kids, and the kids responded well to him being there. But I was surprised by the reactions of others. I was frequently asked, "What does your partner do? What is his *real* job?" And my personal favorite: "He has the dream job, staying at home." Not likely things you would say to a stay-at-home mother.

The hours were much longer at BioSphere. I had to learn how to navigate an organization all over again, while learning about my team, which was much larger and highly skilled. Three months in, I was rethinking my decision. I had had it good at Tri-Go. Was it worth it to leave? Maybe I could go back?

Talking to my mom always helped. I could vent and let out all of the emotion that I was bottling up at work. She listened and calmly said, "Change is hard, Jane. You've got this. Give it some time."

Just when I thought it could not get any worse, Rejen received a promotion to lead the international business and relocated to Hong Kong. I was left without an ally and had a new leader to report to, Steven. The first thing I noticed about Steven was his half-smile. You did not know if he was happy or angry. He did not make eye contact with me, and in meetings he would turn away from me. It was as if I made him uncomfortable. Needless to say, Steven and I did not get along. It felt like either he was out to get me or he wanted to completely avoid me. I couldn't get a read on him, but what I did know was that he did not like me, and it felt personal.

Brad would console me at the end of each day while I admitted my defeats and struggles. He would say, "Give Steven a chance. He is trying to prove himself. Assume positive intent."

While I appreciated Brad's input, I felt he was under-estimating my grim situation. I believed that Steven only wanted me to stay behind the scenes; I would have my team deliver on key tasks, which he then took sole credit for. He was not an inclusive leader. In fact, the only time I had ever met with Steven was in public settings for short periods of time. When I came by his office to talk or ask a question and shut the door, he always asked that it stay open. I did not feel trust with him.

He was holding something back. What was he so afraid of?

After three months of this awkwardness, I decided to have a candid conversation. It reminded me of the one I had with Robert years ago. I was nervous, so I did a power pose (similar to the Superwoman pose) and told myself, *I've got this. The conversation will go well. It will build trust.* The positive thinking skills I had learned from my coach many moons ago came in handy.

I entered Steven's office and closed the door. "We need to talk," I stated firmly, "and we need to talk about something serious with the door closed. I want to have a candid conversation about how we communicate. I do not feel like we trust one another, and it is preventing us from getting work done effectively. I care about this job, and I want to learn how to build trust with you. What do you think?"

Ten seconds of silence passed, and then Steven looked up and made eye contact for the very first time. He said, "I have not worked with a lot of women before, and honestly, you make me nervous. You earned the respect of the team so quickly, I feel like they would rather have you as their leader."

I was stunned. He seemed genuinely intimidated by me. Maybe it was the power pose I did in the bathroom. That stuff really works!

As a smile crossed my lips, I thought I should say something to acknowledge his vulnerability. "I appreciate you sharing that with me. It probably did not feel good to come into a team and not feel welcomed as their leader."

Channeling some Brené Brown, I thought, *Stay in empathy mode. It builds connection. This is not about me. Wait at least seven seconds. Listen and it will come.*

"Yeah, I am struggling to build trust with the team, and I do not know what to do."

"You were put here intentionally to help the organization. I truly believe we are stronger together. I am not ready for the role you have and, actually, have been looking to you to mentor me so I would be ready for it when it is available."

And, then it got real.

"Yeah, I know that, but there is something else. With everything going on in the media, I honestly do not know what to say or do right now. I am afraid of meeting one-on-one with you and other women because people might think something else is going on. That would be harmful for both of our careers. I felt it was easier to meet in public spaces or with the door open."

In my mind, I wanted to run away from this difficult topic. It struck a nerve. Men had been saying things like this casually, like it was okay not to meet with women. I would never think it was okay to not meet one-on-one with men—I would never get my work done!

Instead, I leaned in like Sheryl Sandberg.

"But that is why we have not had *this* conversation. We cannot talk about difficult issues out in the open for anyone to hear and share. And we cannot build trust with the door always open."

"I get it now. Wow, this was a deep conversation. I am glad you shut the door for it. Let's do this more in our one-on-ones. And, let me know more about how I can be a mentor. It would truly be an honor for you to be the natural successor for my role."

We shook hands, and I made sure to look him in the eye and say, "Thank you for the candid conversation. Here's to many more."

We did have many more candid conversations. Steven and I disagreed openly with one another and called each other out for bad behavior. We modeled radical candor and challenging with care for our team to see live. They knew it was safe to share difficult things even if the opinion was unpopular. It did not mean their opinion was the ultimate solution, but it mattered that we heard it before making decisions.

Our team thrived in the coming months and for the balance of that year under our joint leadership. I was the yin to his yang and we complemented one another nicely. I learned a lot from Steven about how to be bold, challenge, and balance my assertiveness while not being too aggressive. He would give me candid feedback after every presentation, in private, and he focused on "do this more…do this less…this is a trick I learned to handle this personality or assertion if you want to try it." He was kind, and he was fair. I was so thankful I had called him out early on in our working relationship. I would have missed out on so much development and would have harbored so much anger.

As I looked around the organization, we were the exception. There were not a lot of inclusive leaders, if any, outside of marketing. The senior leadership changed in the course of just one year after Rejen's departure. Two women left to take positions at other organizations, and what was once 50% women on the leadership team had retracted to 25%. Things were getting worse. Bad behavior like interruptions and yelling became more frequent in leadership team meetings. The sole women leaders were Donna in HR and Karen in diversity and inclusion. Yikes.

I had heard rumblings in the hallways and in talent reviews about open positions: "I am not sure she would *fit* with the team."

What does that mean? I thought in passing.

It was generally echoed with "You know long hours, travel…" Code for excuses.

I would interject and ask, "Have you asked her if she is willing to do those things?" That was usually met with a flinch and eyebrow raise. "Well, no, I guess I could."

This signaled to me that I was less likely to advance into leadership than I had planned. I feared we were backsliding and creating a culture where women were not encouraged to take on senior roles. Steven did not want to lead marketing forever, but I got the feeling that his replacement would be male, despite his dedication to supporting me.

I decided to have another candid conversation. This has become normal, and I liked having them. There was something about the thrill of finding common ground when things seem impossible. I channeled positive intent, thinking, Certainly the CEO wants equality in leadership. He supports women advancing.

I showed up a few minutes early from my scheduled time with Don. Don was a typical CEO on the Fortune 500 list: a neatly groomed middle-aged Caucasian cisgender straight man. He always had a freshly pressed suit on, so I had mirrored his attire with my pantsuit. I detested dressing like this, but I wanted to improve my odds. I had my hair neatly tied back and had worn more makeup than usual to appear as presentable as possible.

I began: "Don, I want to talk to you about something that might be a bit uncomfortable. In my year and a half here, I have noticed that we are not retaining women leaders and people of color at the same rate as the majority group, the white males. I know we are committed to diversity and inclusion, yet I fear there are some underlying behaviors that are preventing us from achieving success. I want you to be honest with me. What do you think?"

There was an uncomfortable silence. It was like a repeat of the first candid conversation that Steven and I had had months earlier.

"I understand. With the losses of Maureen and Terryn, we have a short-term gap. You know that they were very open about why they left. We cannot prevent spouses from leaving for their husband's career or to be with their family more."

It was like he had dropped a hot potato. He left the conversation there for me to pick it up. I was not going to let him off the hook.

"What specifically are we doing to advance more women in leadership? My direct reports and those I mentor are asking me this question, and I do not know how to respond."

"Gender equality is not an issue here. We have had successful women leaders here. It is like if you continuously focus on a problem, you find it everywhere. We just need to focus on what is right for the business, and diversity will come with that."

"Don, I disagree with you. I think our culture is preventing diverse talent from succeeding, and they are leaving because of it. I think we can do better. I want your support to partner with Karen on diversity and inclusion."

Mic dropped. I had asked for it. With my job and reputation on the line, I thought, *What have I done? I am the breadwinner. My family depends on me. What if this is a career-limiting move?*

I was just about to ask to take back what I had said when Don responded. "Okay, go ahead. Make sure it is okay with Steven. I am curious what you come up with."

Don looked down at his watch, probably eager for tee time. I would take this as a small victory, day by day, little by little. I would be a part of the solution, not the problem.

I approached Karen and shared that I was interested in helping her with key initiatives. Steven had taken a project off my plate to free up a few hours a week that I could contribute to the cause. She seemed thankful at first. That was until I shared the idea to have a women's leadership group. I fondly remembered my Tri-Go days and the work we did to build the Women's Leadership Employee Resource Group. We had none of that at BioSphere. It was like I had traveled back in time and things had gotten worse.

She said, "We tried that before, and it was not perceived well. Men felt left out, and when we did include them, they dominated the conversation as if they knew what it was like to be a woman or person of color."

"Well, it sounds like the time to brainstorm new solutions. We need to address the lack of women in leadership and the fact that the number of women advancing in the company is at a five-year low. How about I put together some focus groups to learn more?"

She nodded, then looked back at her computer screen, signaling my dismissal.

I conducted five in-depth focus groups to learn more about the women of BioSphere and their experiences. They candidly shared a wide range of observations.

"There is a boys' club here. My manager will frequently invite the men on my team to go out for beer, watch sports, or play golf, but not me."

"My manager told me he does not ask me to go to lunch with the team because he doesn't want me to feel uncomfortable since I am the only woman."

"My manager walks past my cubicle in the morning and will say hello, but then proceeds to engage in lengthy conversations with only the men about their hobbies."

Afterward, women met with me one-on-one to share more. My mouth dropped in horror as the women openly shared their #metoo experiences, and some stated that nothing had been done about these incidents. To them there was no upside to reporting the incidents to HR. While I was honored they had shared this with me, I felt I had a duty to curb this behavior right away.

Don and Karen were less than supportive about having a #metoo conversation. They felt it was opening a can of worms. They envisioned lawsuits and an exodus of women. I knew they were wrong, so I fought for it. At the next company town hall, Don acknowledged a retreat of women in leadership and said he was committed to making our company a more inclusive workplace for all genders. While he said the right words, he lacked authenticity behind them. They did not feel heartfelt or echo the same sentiment in daily behavior. People did not believe him.

After the disappointing town hall, I knew I had to walk away. I simply did not belong here. After two years of fighting corporate politics, I felt completely defeated. I just couldn't take it anymore, and I left without the prospect of a new job.

My career had been a roller-coaster ride. I was swiftly approaching the mid-career mark and had been a leader at three top-tier companies. I couldn't help but wonder, *Where will I belong?*

Lead Like an Ally Insights

Being an ally is a journey, and organizations with ally curriculums have better business results. Did you catch these insights?

- **Women were dissuaded from meeting with men one-on-one.** Due to fear of sexual harassment accusations and fear of doing or saying the wrong thing, men retreated from one-on-one interactions with women. They were not sure what to say or do, making it easier to withdraw. This is not helpful given that women are nearly 50% of the workforce, and it is unrealistic to avoid 50% of the people you work with. Important conversations took place privately, preventing women from obtaining equal access to those discussions.

- **Jane felt like she did not belong.** Only two of the eight leaders were women, and they were in the traditionally female areas of HR and marketing. Jane is ready to lead but does not see herself reflected in the organization chart. She is stunned to learn that very few women leaders have had success at the company and is fearful that she too will suffer that same fate.

- **Leaders tried to make gender a nonissue.** When the CEO dismisses her observations of the diversity problem, Jane is taken aback, and it stunts her development. She identifies as feminine and wants to bring her full self to work each day. She feels like she has to be a different version of herself to belong and fit in. It is distracting to think continuously about what to wear and what to say and to tone down her emotions.

- **Women received negative feedback that signaled they did not belong.** Saying "I am not sure she would fit with the team" is inappropriate unless it is based on specific job performance criteria. It is likely that because the team has not seen many women leaders do it before, fear of change prevents the team from moving forward. This is a chicken and egg problem. With few women leading, it is hard to see it as possible, yet women need to see what good leadership looks like from the top women leaders in order to believe it is possible for them.

- **There was not a safe place for women to connect.** Beyond physical safety, all genders need to feel psychologically safe at work. There was not a place for women to connect and share experiences and feel seen and heard.

Lead Like an Ally Ideas

- **Address any negativity surrounding the idea of men and women meeting one-on-one.** Women need equal access to decision makers, who often happen to be men. One-on-one meetings, across genders, are unavoidable. If the culture in your workplace is openly discouraging this, address it immediately. If you witness behavior like Steven's, call it out. Practice Flip It to Test It by asking, *If you were meeting with a man, would you question this private meeting?* That usually stops people in their tracks. Private conversations are essential. They are typically where decisions are made that impact the entire organization. Women cannot be left out of those.

- **Encourage women to advance outside of traditionally designated female roles.** The fields of HR and marketing typically have a higher concentration of female employees, whereas engineering, R&D, operations, finance, and sales have a deficit. Challenge the mindset that women will advance in only HR or marketing by providing full access to the cross-functional experience necessary to maneuver throughout the organization.

- **Engage in open dialogue about company problems to fully comprehend why they matter.** While most efforts start with good intentions, sometimes organizations are derailed by pursuing the quick wins. Their focus is directed toward proving they are becoming more inclusive and promoting diversity, but what gets lost in the message is why it matters and they problems they are facing. Glossing over issues that need to be addressed is a critical error. Avoid this mistake by engaging people in real-time dialogues with data illustrating the problem and the "why" behind diversity and inclusion. Make it clear that diversity is not an initiative but rather a cultural shift.

- **Challenge gender bias**. Rather than assume women do not want to travel or are unavailable outside of work, *ask them*. Assuming is benevolent sexism—good intentions but bad behavior. Make a habit of asking, "Did you ask her?" or "I would think she knows she is pregnant; perhaps she does want the promotion."

- **Have an inclusive Employee Resource Group for women**. If your organization has yet to establish a safe place for women to engage in a dialogue about their challenges in the workplace, start one. If you already have one, be sure to have an executive sponsor, a strong mission, goals, and a road map of activities to drive the mission. Pop-up events and book clubs are great but all too often overlooked. Engage men as allies in some, but not all, of the programming. It is important that women of color feel included, so be sure to encourage all women to come.

Manager Tool Kit

You do not have to reinvent the wheel as a manager. There are many excellent resources to support you in your inclusive leadership journey. Inclusive leaders talk candidly about diversity, equality, and inclusion.

Conduct Candid Conversations

Step 1: Assume Positive Intent

It is a lot easier to engage in a candid conversation when you assume your audience has good intentions. Oftentimes, opening the conversation with your own vulnerability helps your audience connect with you on a human level. It builds trust, and if you do not have trust with your audience, it is essential to start there.

Consider opening with "I know this is uncomfortable, but I have something I want to share with you"; "I want our relationship to be better, so I need to share something that is hard for me to say"; or "I want to build more trust with you; what do you think could help us work better together?"

Step 2: Share Feedback

The situation-behavior-impact model of feedback is powerful. Once you have opened the dialogue from a place of positive intent, go into feedback, first framing the situation. A good way to convey the situation is to describe the who, what, where, and when, clearly painting a picture so the person can recall what you are talking about.

After setting up the situation, describe behaviors with statements like "I saw you do this," or "I heard you say this." Recount verbatim what they said, so as to not lose them or create defensiveness. Close with the impact. Cover how this behavior impacts the business, the client, the team, diverse groups, and so on. This will help them understand the negative repercussions of their behavior and how or what they need to modify to avoid this in the future. Change becomes possible once someone has the opportunity to fully process their situation.

Step 3: Coach to Success

Another proven model for candid conversations is asking coaching questions. I use the GROW model with my clients: goal, reality, options, will. In each phase you have a variety of questions on deck to guide the conversation. You want to engage your audience within five minutes of the candid conversation with incisive, open-ended questions.

Consider these coaching questions:

- **Goal:** What does success look like? What do you think? What do you want?
- **Reality:** What is happening now? What are the barriers to success? What is preventing us from being successful together?
- **Options:** Let's brainstorm solutions. What is a wild idea? What if you could wave a magic wand and make it better, what would we do?
- **Will:** What did we decide to do today? What action steps are we committing to? How do we want me to hold one another accountable?

It is important to spend time on reality and will. People usually jump to the options that do not address the root cause of the issue, making the issue likely to surface again. Follow-up is the key to success, so be prepared to inspect what you expect.

Chapter 6

MEASURE SUCCESS

I felt as though I had been chewed up and spit out by corporate America, where I no longer belonged. What is next? I had no job but wanted to be a part of the solution.

These thoughts spun in my mind like a tornado, circling and circling.

I hired a career coach to help me map out my next steps. Brenda had done her time in corporate America, and her career path closely resembled mine. She had made her exit a bit earlier than I and started her own coaching practice. I admired her courage to go out on her own, something I lacked at the moment.

I knew I needed to be brave. I had taken a big leap leaving BioSphere with no known prospects on the horizon. Brad was supportive, and we were able to spend more time together as a family, which was therapeutic. How could I look at Lucy's and Cole's little faces and not feel a sense of purpose? I was lucky to have my family. I became determined to ensure my work aligned with genuine purpose: to support them.

In our first coaching session, Brenda walked me through my 360 leadership assessment results. It was eye-opening to see my strengths, challenges, and opportunities all in one document. I had scored highly in inclusiveness and pioneering as a leader. My strengths were clear: confidence and being more decisive as a leader.

My confidence had been strong earlier in my career, but it had disappeared. *Where had it gone?* I posed this question to Brenda. She stated it was a commonality in many of the women she coached. The bravery and courage we once had is often tempered by non-inclusive work environments, which teach us to hold back. Women are often judged differently from their male counterparts when exhibiting the very same behaviors. She said it was called unconscious bias.

She then asked me about my experiences in the workplace. What kind of feedback I had received on performance reviews? How did people react to my ideas in meetings? As I reflected, I recalled times when people questioned my authority to make decisions or said that I was too outspoken. In response to this, I had conditioned myself over time to temper my confidence to fit in. When I had been decisive, people questioned my authority, saying, "Are you sure? Whose decision is this to make?" as though I were not a real leader.

Brenda decided we should focus on my confidence and courage as our two strategies to work on in our time together. I built positive affirmations and wrote a story of my future self. It was so helpful to not feel like I was alone. Each week, we met via video call. Changing behavior is hard. The strategies that I worked on did not come easily at first. I had a lot of self-doubt and a lot of fears to unpack. Yet, over time, I did improve. I was stepping back into who I was meant to be, and it helped a great deal to be out of a toxic work environment.

Once I had my confidence back, we worked on my career path options. Brenda asked me to reflect on my very best days at work: What was I doing? How did I feel? Who was I with? Then, she asked me to think about the skills that came easily to me. What did people ask for my help with frequently? What did I do efficiently and with high quality? What was I doing when time seemed to fly by?

I brainstormed two categories: my skills and my wills. At the top of my skills list was creative problem solving, crafting a vision, building business plans, facilitating collaboration, and ideation. I was strong at these skills, and when doing these activities I felt the most energized and connected with myself. I preferred workplace cultures that were inclusive, where I could work with people who were different than me and whom I could learn from, and being a leader who drives positive change. I needed a mission that I connected with on a deep level. I had to have a purpose in my work. These were nonnegotiable values I craved from the workplace.

Self-reflection is powerful. It aided me in efficiently executing my wills list. I could easily comb through job roles and responsibilities to weed out what was a fit and what did not, and then research the prospective company to see if they were aligned with my values. I began conducting interviews to learn more about specific job areas. The top three roles that matched my skills and wills were nonprofit leader, corporate social responsibility leader, and diversity and inclusion leader. As I shared these options with those I met, they offered insights into open roles and organizations that were looking for this type of talent.

Opportunities poured in from both coasts, but not from Chicago, our home for nearly two decades. The Midwest is infamous for its "culture of nice," which I believed held many organizations back from truly being progressive. As I traveled, I saw the same issues in New York and California; however, there organizations were leaning in hard to the candid conversation rather than glossing over diversity and inclusion.

Brenda helped me prepare for my interviews by acting as a sounding board as I vetted options with her. When the offers started coming in, my confidence grew. People wanted me, and I had a purpose. I could add value to an organization. I finally belonged.

In the end, I narrowed it down to the two best options: a chief equality officer role at a marketing agency in New York or a local nonprofit executive director role in Chicago.

I mapped out the pros and cons with Brenda, and it became crystal clear that a move was necessary. I was going to uproot my family to New York to pursue my dream. I had always wanted to work on workplace culture from the front line, and as the very first equality leader at this organization, I had white space to play with to create an inclusive culture from the ground up.

Two months later, my family was on an airplane heading east. I was bursting with enthusiasm. We settled into our new home in the suburbs, and I took the train into the city each day, using that time to reflect on and build my ideas and plans.

The first day at Octiv was a whirlwind. I was introduced to what felt like a thousand people, and I was very much drinking from the proverbial fire hose. There were lots of suggestions about what my role should be focused on and lots of ideas to consider. I valued the energy for the role, yet knew balancing all the perspectives would be challenging. I was certainly up for that challenge.

The first week was strictly orientation. I got my computer, attended the mandatory trainings, and met my team. The following week, I mapped out my onboarding plan with input from the senior leadership team (which I was now on—wow!). It felt good to be with a team that had diversity. Of the eight senior leaders, there were three women and two people of color. Our chief operations officer was also disabled. I had never been on a team with that kind of diversity. Yet, there are always opportunities to be better.

I met one-on-one with each leader that week and asked similar questions of each: Why do diversity and inclusion matter? How are we measuring success on diversity? What have we done in the past to support inclusion? What worked? What didn't work?

Their answers revealed a wide variety of challenges. It was disappointing that not one single leader had a good story about why diversity and inclusion mattered. Their business case was cited at times, knowing that diverse teams outperform those that are not diverse. Their human case was unclear, and there had to be more emotion around it for this to be taken seriously; otherwise, it just felt like a flavor-of-the-month program. In addition, there were no metrics for success. I could not believe that there were no means to set goals or measure progress, given the diversity of the senior leadership team. As I looked down through the organization, there was a glaring gap in middle management. Many of our recent promotions and front line hires were notably not diverse. The diverse talent pipeline was not there, and that would be a big problem in two years if we did nothing. As I dug deeper, the middle managers got defensive when asked about their hiring decisions and how they managed the performance of their team. They would respond with statements like "I am not going to hire diverse talent just to hire diverse talent. They have to be equally qualified. I am not going to lower my standards. We have a job to do."

That was biased. *Why did they assume diverse talent is somehow not as qualified?*

The first 90 days were all about fact-finding. I identified the top five challenges and presented them to the leadership team:

1. There was no "why" for diversity.
2. We had no plan for it.
3. Leadership was not being held accountable for inclusion.
4. Leadership lacked the skills to be inclusive.
5. There was a lack of transparency around diversity.

To address these challenges, I leveraged my creative problem-solving and strong facilitation skills to engage the team. I wanted the ideas to be their own and for them to feel like a part of it. It was important that we modeled inclusive behavior, as our very purpose was to increase inclusion and equality.

The first town hall discussion was healthy. Teams leaned in to the candid conversation. I engaged them in a discussion about why diversity matters to them personally, and we bubbled up the answers to craft a succinct statement that would be our rallying cry for equality: "We value diversity, equality, and inclusion because we care about all humans. We believe our culture is one where all people can be seen and heard equally. We want our team to reflect our clients and marketplace equally."

After two hours of rich discussion, I was left to wordsmith the statement and market it externally. It was fun to see the team come to life as they personally connected with the message. It was not about me; it was about the team. I was proud to work with this group of leaders. I realized it was the first time I felt that way about my work and team. I could bring my whole self to work. I truly belonged.

Next came the plan. For this, I engaged all people leaders in the organization. We had just shy of 1,000 total employees and 55 people leaders, a ratio I suspected was off. We needed more leaders. Many were overwhelmed in their regular duties to have the capacity to lead their team. I was met with constant excuses about not having the time to do the equality work. They would complain, "Diversity and inclusion is not my job," and "I do not want to have this on my performance review." Their resistance to change was alarming. It did not feel right to me.

I knew, from my past experience of facilitating change with the product launch, that this was step 1: resistance. People do not like to change. That is why I started with the why. You have to have a strong "why" for change and translate that into "what's in it for me?" I met individually with all 55 people leaders and asked them to share their thoughts. Where did they need support? How would diversity help them as a leader? How did they prefer to engage in the discussion?

Some conversations were better than others. Every leader was at a different spot on the journey to being an inclusive leader. I listened for clues on where they were. I estimated 20% to be firmly resistant "not my job" people, 60% squarely in the middle "I don't know what to do or say" people, and the 20% balance were fully onboard as allies. I chose to focus on the murky middle.

We developed an inclusive leadership education program that met our allies where they were. I focused on key pillars I knew to be true of inclusive cultures based on my research and benchmarking with other equality officers around the globe. The plan was intentional. It provided focus on key behaviors that every people leader could take to be an ally for equality. We called the program Lead Like an Ally. It was a 52-week program aimed at elevating inclusive leadership skills. Given time constraints, I knew the half-day and full-day workshop approach would not work. We needed real-time tools to have intentional inclusive conversations. I needed to make sure every leader was held accountable for being inclusive—a tall order.

I built a scorecard to support the education initiative with key measures of success. We mapped our leadership competencies to the prioritized inclusive behaviors: coaching, giving and receiving feedback, being curious, practicing the growth mindset, and addressing bias. These pillars then became the foundation for our inclusive leadership journey. Each week every leader would receive an email with a new tool to learn via video and a worksheet to complete. Then every month we held a town hall meeting for those leaders to discuss what they were learning and to share their workbook activities. It was highly encouraged, but not mandatory.

We averaged 80% in attendance during the first three months. The resisters were still refusing to show up, and they had a variety of excuses ranging from illness to conflicting priorities. I met with each of the resisters, one-on-one, to ask for feedback on the program: What did they want more of? What did they want less of? I got the feeling that they just wanted it to go away.

This was the toughest part. I had to have candid conversations with the managers overseeing the middle management resisters to ask them to hold them accountable. Some were willing, but others were not, citing high performance as the defense. I explained it did not matter if they were getting results if they were not doing it in an inclusive manner. I surfaced this feedback with the leadership team. They did not like what I had to say.

Many recoiled and crossed their arms to signal disapproval. I asked for permission to put each non-ally on a performance improvement plan. I was met with silence. We had done all the work to commit to equality, and when push came to shove, they did not want to do the hard work to get there. I felt like my hands were tied. What could I do?

I resorted to positive peer pressure. I asked the people leaders who were actively participating in the series to share their experiences with those that were not attending. They slowly started to join the monthly discussions, and I saw them engaging on the learning platform more. We now hovered around 90% who had engaged in some form. The bottom 10% had to go, in my opinion. It simply was not okay to let bad behavior continue.

With a 10% increase that quarter, I had a business case to now share with the leadership team. I wrestled with how to get them on board with holding the remaining 10% accountable. They held back at first, but then, as I began to share success stories of those participating, they let go of the notion that losing a few team members was a bad thing. It was actually a good thing. We could not move forward unless every leader was on board.

In partnership with each leader's manager, we engaged in candid conversations and drew a line in the sand for the leader. They were on notice that if they chose not to engage in the next quarter, they no longer would be employed with us. Eyebrows were raised and people got angry, but then they started coming. They realized that the tools were helping them be a better leader and made their jobs easier.

A year into the program, we were at a 95% participation rate. The bottom 5% were let go, and that is when the momentum took off. We were being more candid than we ever had been. People leaders were surfacing bad behavior on their teams, and we were recruiting more diverse talent as a result. Stay interviews revealed that employee engagement was at an all-time high, and we had corrected the leaky bucket of diverse talent exiting at a higher rate than the majority groups. We promoted more women and culturally diverse people into leadership roles, and the flywheel was spinning. We became known as the marketing agency in New York City to work for. I was asked to speak at national diversity, equality, and inclusion conferences.

I was the happiest I have ever been at home and at work. I was elated with my team. I had the dream job, and it was all because we created an intentional plan with focused behaviors that we held our leaders accountable to. We made tough choices to lose good yet non-inclusive leaders. We set a serious tone for equality.

I do this work because it matters. I did not have to do it alone, for I had a team around me that were leading like allies.

I was home, at last.

Lead Like an Ally Insights

Being an ally is a journey, and organizations with ally curriculums have better business results. Did you catch these insights?

- **Leadership did not define why inclusion matters and what it means.** The organization stated that inclusion and gender equality were important yet did not provide specifics. It is important to know why it matters—the business case, the human element, personal reasons—and what the plan is.

- **There were no metrics to measure success.** Any initiative that is important in business is measured. Without clear goals to show how inclusion is important, it signals that it is not.

- **There was zero transparency about where the gaps were.** When asked about goals and data, the leadership team's responses were evasive and defensive. They did not lean into the difficult conversation out of fear of doing or saying the wrong thing. This teaches people that it is not okay to talk about these difficult issues openly and stirs private conversations that lead to a more toxic culture with lower trust.

- **There was a lack of intentionality.** There was no series of intentional activities to close gaps on equality in the organization. While the leadership team

was well versed in the language and behaviors surrounding diversity, equality, and inclusion, middle
management was forgotten.

- **Leaders were not held accountable for metrics on
their team.** It is critical that leaders are accountable
for inclusive leadership behaviors and metrics to
avoid passing blame and excuses for non-inclusive
cultures and behaviors.

Lead Like an Ally Ideas

- **Start with the "why."** For any business initiative to
matter, people have to be engaged in why it matters.
It is not the "what" or "how" that motivates people to
change. Get your team together and craft a statement
of purpose for diversity, equality, and inclusion and
why it matters to you. Make sure to include every
employee and communicate it both externally and
internally remind people of the "why."

- **Create a dashboard.** Metrics matter. Make sure
inclusive leadership skills, behaviors, and key activities are being tracked starting with recruitment and
continuing through hiring, promoting, and separat-
ing. Consider the full employee life cycle and where
diverse talent is thriving and not thriving, and hold
each leader accountable for their metrics.

- **Share the dashboard regularly.** Good leaders inspect
what they expect. If you measure key behaviors and
business metrics, share them openly and often. Have

ongoing conversations about what leaders are doing to drive equality in the workplace and coach them to success if they are not engaging in positive behavior.

- **Create an inclusive leader program.** Define the key behaviors of inclusive leadership and educate leaders on them. Meet them where they are at with tools to be better.

- **Have zero tolerance for non-inclusive behavior.** If leaders refuse to step up, call them out and ask them to join. Create a culture where positive peer pressure spreads and all leaders want to be a part of inclusion.

Manager Tool Kit

You do not have to reinvent the wheel as a manager. There are excellent resources to support you in your inclusive leadership journey. Inclusive leaders talk candidly about diversity, equality, and inclusion.

Launch a Lead Like an Ally Program

Today's leader must be inclusive, but many do not know what to do or how to implement it. That is why having a step-by-step program can meet them precisely where they are at on their ally journey.

Consider the following skills as starting points for your own program.

Skill 1: Self-Awareness

- Know your ally "why"

- Set a vision
- Prepare a SWOT analysis (strengths, weaknesses, opportunities, and threats)
- Have an allyship plan

Skill 2: Self-Management
- Practice empathy
- Strengthen emotional intelligence
- Be vulnerable
- Seek to understand

Skill 3: Comfort with Discomfort
- Challenge with care
- Give and take feedback
- Conduct candid conversations
- Unpack privilege

Skill 4: Your Ally Role
- Identify the ally continuum
- Mentor
- Step up as a sponsor
- Coach to success
- Advocate for others

Skill 5: Space for Others
- Stay open to input
- Be curious
- Have inclusive meetings

- Practice perspective taking
- Help others be seen and heard

Skill 6: *Your Diversity Story*
- Think of a time when you were different
- Understand covering
- Write out the story
- Share the story

Skill 7: *Leadership Style*
- Know when to ask versus to tell
- Delegate
- Know the GROW model
- Give to give
- Identify strengths in others
- Bolster the confidence of others

Skill 8: *Unconscious Bias*
- Check unconscious bias
- Call out microaggressions
- Know the science of bias
- Limit "othering" people

Skill 9: *Gender*
- Stop benevolent sexism
- Know gender bias
- Model inclusive parental leave
- Be clear about sexual harassment policies

Skill 10: Race

- Own your role in the system
- Address not seeing color
- Focus on cultural diversity
- Use the term *people of color*

Skill 11: LGTQ

- Learn about the gender spectrum
- Facilitate being out at work
- Use the term *partner*
- Ask about others' experiences

Skill 12: Build Sustainable Systems

- Ensure interview slates are diverse
- Measure progress on equality
- Broaden diversity to more than race and gender
- Set expectations for leaders to care

CONCLUSION: WHAT NOW?

Today's workplace was designed by men for men to succeed. The same rules that work for men do not work for women. Coupled with the fact that gender-equal and diverse teams outperform nondiverse (primarily white male) teams on innovation, decision making, and profitability and that organizations must engage all talent to be successful in the future, this indicates that the rules need to change.

Organizations need to be more inclusive to attract and engage diverse talent. Simply recruiting diverse talent will not close the diversity gap. Women and otherwise diverse talent want to work for organizations that value them, where they find purpose in their work, and they are seen, heard, and feel that they belong.

Now is the time for equality for all.

Now is the time for allies for equality.

Now is the time to rewrite Jane's story.

As you have read the story of Jane, think about the young women in your life. Ask yourself, Am I okay with this narrative playing out for them?

When I look at my daughter, Jane, and all young women I know personally and professionally, my eyes brim with tears thinking of this scenario panning out for the next generation. It was not okay for me, and it is definitely not okay for them. Gender equality is forecasted to be achieved in 2080, when my daughter will be 67. While I hope that I am still around promoting equality in the workplace, I do not want her to have to wait that long for her turn to be equal.

I will tell her it will be harder for her, that she will have to work harder than her male counterparts just because she is a woman. While I will acknowledge that she should not have to do so, this is where we are now. And, we can only get better.

For me, this is personal. Make it personal for you.

When my mother told me that feminists had paved the way for all women to succeed growing up, I believed her. She would say, "Everything is equal now." She was a single mother, and I saw her do everything. I did not see gender in my house growing up. She did both the traditional male and female roles. Imagine my surprise when I entered corporate America in 2004 and was met with an all-male team of colleagues and an organization chart where no one looked like me. The one token woman in the C-suite looked like a man and acted like one, too.

Those who are allies in training love to defend themselves: "We have a meritocracy where hard work is rewarded, and we are not going to lower our standards to attract women and otherwise diverse talent."

I respond to this with my road analogy. Imagine a road, one built by white men for white men to succeed. It is cleanly paved, has no potholes, and is easy to navigate. That is what the workplace is like for white men. Now, imagine that same road with little potholes along the way, perhaps a speed bump here and there, with poor lighting at night and very few street signs to navigate the way. That is what it is like to be a woman or person of color. See, when the system is built for one type of person to succeed, it is institutionalized for others to not succeed.

In other words, the workplace is not a meritocracy. Hard work is not always rewarded. Unconscious bias is everywhere, along with microaggressions against people of color and women that prevent them from succeeding. In fact, saying that we will not lower our standards to attract diverse talent signals a biased belief that diverse talent is somehow not as talented.

My hope is that as you read Jane's story, you saw the little potholes and speed bumps along the way, the subtle biased behaviors and microaggressions that signaled that she was different, did not belong, or had to alter herself to fit in at work. For men, these things are hard to see. We cannot change our own privilege. We can unpack it, though. We can choose to see the differences in how we are treated as compared to others. Spend a day observing women and how they are treated at work compared to their male colleagues. Be curious. Watch to see if they are interrupted in meetings, if men take credit for their ideas, or if assumptions are made about her parental responsibilities. While I hope that you do not see these behaviors, I bet you will.

Then, it is your choice to do something about it.

My goal in writing this was to meet men where they are at in a safe, nonconfrontational style. This story does not have to be true for future women leaders. It is changing every day. I believe that our allies will help us move faster down the road to equality. Once our allies see the potholes and subtle setbacks, they can fill the potholes and help clear the obstacles preventing us from being successful. If you see something, say something. Do not be a bystander. Now that you know what to look for, when you see it, lean into a candid conversation. If Jane can do it, you can do it.

Assuming most of you reading this book are women (I get it!), share this book with a man you know who could benefit from being an ally for equality. Ask him to read a chapter and see if he caught the insights at the end, and what he thought of the ideas. See if you can have a candid conversation as Jane did with her allies and non-allies. We have to meet our allies where they are. If we are waiting for men to be perfect, we will wait forever. Let's invite them into the dialogue and educate them on their imperfections in candid, safe ways.

I do this work because equality is important. I have to be a part of this conversation. I invite you to be a more vocal part of this conversation in your organization and social circles or—even better—share this message publicly with the hashtags #womensleadership, #alliesforequality, #genderequality, or one of your liking. Share our mantra: "I believe we are stronger together. We are ONE." Be brave. Do it for the young women and all the women you know.

Share your ally stories and connect with me on my website (www.NextPivotPoint.com) and on social media @nextpivotpoint.

ACKNOWLEDGMENTS

I have had many allies in writing, editing, and providing input into this work. First, thank you for my ally, Nicola Evans, who coined the first version of this title and combed over every page of this book. Her critical eye and perceptive curiosity made this better. We have been best friends since the sixth grade, and I have trusted her judgment immensely with this work. As a mother of twin girls and an immigrant to this country, she has a unique perspective and shared passion for this work. I value her.

Thank you to all of my beta readers: Gretchen Schott, Rachel Pritz, Joseph Moheban, and Neilia Brown. I appreciate your candor and reading and sharing what you liked and would like to see more of and less of. Feedback is a gift, and you certainly delivered.

Last, yet not least, thank you to my ally, Jenni Robbins. She lent me the courage to write this book and introduced me to the Morgan James Publishing family to make it happen. I am thankful for your immense support.

LEAD LIKE AN ALLY: HINDSIGHT IS 20/20, A 12-MONTH GUIDE TO BEING AN INCLUSIVE LEADER

So, what about those middle managers who liked the tool kits at the end of each chapter, yet want more?

I have a solution. My Lead Like an Ally program starts in 2020. Today's C-suite executives and front-line employees are being educated on diversity, equality, and inclusion. The manager who has been with the organization for 5–20 years is often forgotten, and they are responsible for hiring, promotion, performance management, and separation decisions—essentially, the entire employee experience. We have to start there.

Educating middle managers on what takes to Lead Like an Ally is pivotal for gender equality and overall diversity and inclusion. The Lead Like an Ally online learning portal has 52 weeks of content that takes managers no more than an hour a month to complete. This micro-learning approach ensures that the real learning happens with the application in everyday scenarios. It comes with a comprehensive workbook to guide their allyship journey.

Each week, a new module guides managers through a key skill, starting with self-awareness and their personal "why" for being an ally, through uncovering unconscious bias and creating sustainable systems for positive culture change.

Do you want to be an ally for equality? Those across the gender spectrum can benefit from this ongoing conversation. You can have more candid conversations, and you do not have to do it alone.

Learn more about www.nextpivotpoint.com/lead-like-an-ally.

MANAGER CHECKLIST

I n reading this book, you likely got a lot of ideas to "Lead Like an Ally," and perhaps feel overwhelmed with what to do first. To those that value simplicity, I offer these ideas to consider as a menu to prioritize and take action on.

Lead Like an Ally: Hindsight Is 2020, a 52-Week Guide to Being an Inclusive Leader

- Know your ally "why"
- Set a vision for what it means to be an ally for you (mentor, sponsor, advocate, coach, challenge)
- Prepare your ally SWOT analysis (strengths, weaknesses, opportunities, and threats)
- Have an allyship plan (goals and action steps)

- Practice empathy
- Strengthen emotional intelligence
- Be vulnerable
- Seek to understand versus to be understood
- Challenge with care
- Give and take feedback
- Conduct candid conversations
- Unpack privilege
- Identify the ally continuum (apathy, awareness, activity, advocacy)
- Mentor different people
- Step up as a sponsor
- Coach to success
- Advocate for others
- Stay open to input
- Be curious
- Have inclusive meetings
- Practice perspective taking
- Help others be seen and heard
- Think of a time when you were different
- Understand covering
- Write out your ally story
- Share your ally story
- Know when to ask versus to tell
- Delegate
- Know the GROW model
- Give to give versus give to get
- Identify strengths in others

- Bolster the confidence of others
- Check unconscious bias
- Call out microaggressions
- Know the science of bias
- Limit "othering" people
- Stop benevolent sexism
- Know gender bias
- Model inclusive parental leave
- Be clear about sexual harassment policies
- Own your role in the system
- Address not seeing color
- Focus on cultural diversity
- Use the term *people of color*
- Learn about the gender spectrum
- Facilitate being out at work
- Use the term *partner*
- Ask about others' experiences
- Ensure interview slates are diverse
- Measure progress on equality
- Broaden diversity to more than race and gender
- Set expectations for leaders to lead like allies

ABOUT THE AUTHOR

Julie Kratz is a highly acclaimed leadership trainer who leads teams and produces real results in corporate America. After experiencing her own career "pivot point," Julie developed a process for women leaders to build winning game plans. She lends her expertise around gender equality and leadership as a keynote speaker, workshop facilitator, and executive coach. Julie has a MBA from the Kelley School of Business at Indiana University is a Certified Master Coach as well as Certified Unconscious Bias Trainer. Learn more at NextPivotPoint.com.